How to prepare for the Exam, and how to use this book.

When I study for an exam I break things my studying down into three steps. First I read a text book. Second I find a video course to go through the material a second time in another format. And Third I Find whatever practice question I can and practice until I know the material inside and out. This book is intended to be more practice questions than anyone would ever need to pass the CompTIA Security+ exam. And with so many questions focusing on Domain 5 alone is more than anyone should ever need to blow the test out of the water.

For step one I created a text book that goes over each testable aspect of the exam individually to make grasping the material easy. It's from Yavoz.tech titled "CompTIA Security+ 701 Made Easy" to build a strong understanding of the material.
https://www.amazon.com/CompTIA-Security-701-Made-Easy/dp/B0CNBM5K2Y/ref=sr_1_1?crid=1AJKC3Q108CSH&keyw ords=kie+yavorsky&qid=1700611266&sprefix=kie+yavorsky%2C aps%2C84&sr=8-1

This will provide a solid foundation in cybersecurity concepts and practices. After going through a good textbook it's time for step two. A great free video course is offered on YouTube.com from Professor Messer. Go watch his course.

https://www.youtube.com/watch?v=KiEptGbnEBc&list=PLG49S3 nxzAnI4QDVqK-hOnoqcSKEIDDuv

Visual and auditory reinforcement through video content can help solidify your understanding of the material. Finally, the last step, step three is to find practice questions like the ones in this book to test and assess your knowledge and identify any areas that you may need to further review. That's all there is to it, simple and straight to the point. **Now Let's Get to some Practice Questions! Good Luck!**

Domain 4.0 Security Operations

1. You are a security administrator in a large organization. The company is in the process of implementing a new security governance framework. Which of the following is the most important benefit of having a well-defined security governance framework?

    A) Ensuring compliance with industry regulations
    B) Minimizing the impact of security incidents
    C) Streamlining the security budget allocation
    D) Improving employee awareness of security best practices

Correct Answer: A) Ensuring compliance with industry regulations
Explanation: A well-defined security governance framework is crucial for ensuring that the organization complies with relevant industry regulations and standards. It provides a structured approach to managing and controlling security-related processes, which is essential for meeting legal and regulatory requirements.

2. As part of the security governance process, a company is conducting a risk assessment to identify and prioritize potential security threats. Which of the following activities is typically performed during a risk assessment?

    A) Developing security policies
    B) Implementing intrusion detection systems
    C) Identifying vulnerabilities and their potential impact
    D) Configuring firewall rules

Correct Answer: C) Identifying vulnerabilities and their potential impact Explanation: During a risk assessment, the focus is on identifying and analyzing potential vulnerabilities and their impact on the organization's assets. This process helps in prioritizing the most critical risks and determining appropriate risk mitigation strategies.

3. A company is implementing a new security governance policy. They want to ensure that all employees are aware of the policy and acknowledge their understanding and compliance. Which of the following methods should the company use to achieve this?

A. Send an email to all employees with the policy attached
B. Conduct a training session and have employees sign an acknowledgment form
C. Post the policy on the company's intranet site
D. Have a manager verbally communicate the policy to their team

Correct Answer: B. Explanation: Conducting a training session and having employees sign an acknowledgment form ensures that the policy is not only communicated but also that employees confirm their understanding and commitment to comply with it.

4. A multinational corporation is establishing security governance policies for its various branches across different countries. Which of the following actions should the corporation take to ensure compliance with local regulations and laws?

A. Create a single global policy for all branches to follow
B. Hire a legal team to review and approve the policies
C. Consult with legal experts in each country to tailor the policies
D. Implement the policies without considering local regulations

Correct Answer: C. Explanation: Consulting with legal experts in each country to tailor the policies will ensure that the corporation's security governance policies comply with local regulations and laws in each specific location.

5. A company has noticed an increase in security incidents related to unauthorized access. Which of the following security governance policies should the company prioritize to address this issue?

A. Access control and identity management
B. Data encryption for sensitive information
C. Incident response and management
D. Security awareness training for employees

Correct Answer: A. Explanation: Prioritizing access control and identity management policies will help address the issue of unauthorized access by implementing measures to authenticate and authorize users' access to resources.

6. After a security breach, a company is reviewing its security governance policies. Which of the following should be included in the post-incident review to improve the policies?

A. Conducting a comprehensive security training for all employees
B. Implementing stricter physical access controls
C. Identifying gaps in the existing policies and procedures
D. Increasing the budget for security technologies

Correct Answer: C. Explanation: Identifying gaps in the existing policies and procedures is essential for improving security governance policies after a security breach, as it allows the company to address weaknesses and enhance its overall security posture.

7. An employee at a company frequently uses their work computer to visit social media sites and stream videos during office hours. Which of the following best describes this behavior in relation to the company's AUP?

A. Acceptable
B. Unacceptable
C. Conditional
D. Recommended

Correct Answer: B. Explanation:
Visiting social media sites and streaming videos during office hours typically violates an AUP as it can impact productivity and pose security risks to the company's network and data.

8. A new intern connects their personal laptop to the company's guest Wi-Fi network and starts running a gaming server for personal use. What should the company's IT security team do?

   A. Allow it, as it's on the guest network
   B. Monitor the activity and inform the intern about the AUP
   C. Immediately block the intern's device from the network
   D. Ask the intern to pay for the extra network usage

Correct Answer: C. Explanation: Running a gaming server on the company's network, even the guest network, is a violation of the AUP and should be addressed by immediately blocking the intern's device from the network to prevent further policy violations.

9. A company is implementing a new information security policy. They want to ensure that employees understand the policy and agree to adhere to it. Which of the following should the company use to achieve this?

   A. Security awareness training
   B. Network access control
   C. Intrusion detection system
   D. Biometric authentication

Correct Answer: A. Explanation: Security awareness training is essential for ensuring that employees understand the information security policy and know how to adhere to it. It educates employees about security threats, best practices, and their responsibilities, ultimately helping to create a security-conscious culture within the organization.

10. A company is drafting an acceptable use policy (AUP) as part of its information security framework. Which of the following should be addressed in the AUP?

A. Procedures for responding to security incidents
B. Guidelines for classifying sensitive information
C. Specifications for network bandwidth allocation
D. Rules for reporting software bugs and glitches

Correct Answer: B. Explanation: An acceptable use policy (AUP) typically includes guidelines for classifying sensitive information and outlines how this information should be handled, stored, and transmitted. This helps employees understand their responsibilities in safeguarding sensitive data and contributes to overall data protection.

11. In the event of a natural disaster, a company's business continuity policy dictates the activation of its off-site recovery site. Which of the following concepts does this policy primarily address?

A. Redundancy
B. Single point of failure
C. Mean time to repair
D. Recovery time objective

Correct Answer: D. Explanation: The activation of an off-site recovery site is related to the recovery time objective (RTO), which defines the targeted duration for restoring a system after a disruption. This policy aims to minimize downtime and maintain business continuity.

12. As part of its business continuity plan, a company implements a hot site to ensure continuous operations in the event of a data center failure. Which of the following best describes a hot site?

A. A fully equipped data center with real-time replication of critical systems and data
B. A secondary facility with basic infrastructure and limited resources
C. A cloud-based backup service for data and applications
D. A contractual agreement with another organization for mutual support during emergencies

Correct Answer: A. Explanation: A hot site is a fully equipped data center with real-time replication of critical systems and data, allowing for seamless transition and minimal downtime in the event of a disaster.

13. A company's disaster recovery plan includes regular backups of all critical data to an off-site location. Which of the following components of the plan does this describe?

A) Business impact analysis
B) Recovery time objective
C) Off-site data storage
D) High availability

Correct Answer: C) Off-site data storage. Explanation: Off-site data storage involves keeping backups of critical data at a location separate from the primary site. This is a key component of a disaster recovery plan to ensure that data can be recovered in case of a site-wide disaster.

14. During a routine security audit, an unauthorized access attempt is detected. What is the next step according to the incident response policy?

A) Implement additional security controls
B) Report the incident to the appropriate authorities
C) Analyze the extent of the unauthorized access attempt
D) Restore affected systems from backup

Correct Answer: C. Explanation: After detecting an unauthorized access attempt, the next step is to analyze the extent of the attempt. Understanding the scope of the incident is crucial before taking further actions such as implementing additional security controls, reporting to authorities, or restoring systems from backup.

15. You are a security analyst in a software development company. During which phase of the Software Development Life Cycle (SDLC) should security requirements be identified and documented?

A. Planning phase
B. Design phase
C. Implementation phase
D. Testing phase

Correct Answer: A. Explanation: During the planning phase of the SDLC, security requirements should be identified and documented to ensure that security is integrated into the project from the beginning. This helps in avoiding costly rework and security vulnerabilities later in the development process.

16. You are the security administrator for a large organization. A request has been made to update the operating system on all employee workstations. Which of the following should be the FIRST step in the change management process?

A) Notify all employees about the upcoming change
B) Perform a risk assessment of the proposed change
C) Obtain approval from the IT director
D) Create a back-out plan in case the update causes issues
Correct

Answer: B. Explanation: Before any change is implemented, it is essential to perform a risk assessment to identify potential impacts and mitigate any associated risks. This aligns with the best practices of change management, ensuring that the proposed change is thoroughly evaluated before moving forward.

17. An organization wants to improve password security. Which of the following is the best approach to achieve this?

A. Allowing employees to write down their passwords
B. Implementing multi-factor authentication
C. Enforcing a minimum password age
D. Allowing the reuse of previous passwords

Correct Answer: B. Explanation: Implementing multi-factor authentication provides an additional layer of security beyond just a password. This significantly enhances password security compared to the other options.

18. A company is concerned about password strength. Which of the following is the most effective way to measure password strength?

A. Using a password blacklist
B. Implementing biometric authentication
C. Conducting regular password audits
D. Calculating entropy of passwords

Correct Answer: D. Explanation: Calculating entropy of passwords provides a quantitative measure of password strength, taking into account factors such as length, character set, and unpredictability. This is more effective than the other options for measuring password strength.

19. When conducting access control testing, which of the following questions is most relevant to understanding the user access provisioning process?

A. What is the process to validate user's identities prior to access being provisioned?
B. Who is responsible for understanding which privacy laws and regulations an agent or broker is subject to?
C. How are super user activities monitored and alerted if access is provisioned outside of the process?
D. Can you explain the user access provisioning process?

Correct Answer: D Explanation: Understanding the user access provisioning process is essential in access control testing, and asking for an explanation of this process provides valuable insights into how an organization manages user access

20. A company is implementing physical security measures for its data center. Which of the following controls would best prevent unauthorized individuals from tailgating into the data center?

A. Mantraps
B. Biometric locks
C. Security cameras
D. Access control lists

Correct Answer: A. Explanation: Mantraps are designed to allow only one person to enter at a time, thereby preventing unauthorized individuals from tailgating. This control is effective in restricting access to sensitive areas such as data centers.

21. A company wants to enhance the security of its premises. Which of the following controls can help in detecting and recording any unauthorized access attempts?

A. Security guards
B. Access logs
C. Intrusion detection systems
D. Biometric access control

Correct Answer: C. Explanation: Intrusion detection systems are designed to detect and record unauthorized access attempts. They can trigger alarms and provide real-time alerts, allowing for a quick response to security breaches.

22. You are configuring a VPN for remote access to the corporate network. Which of the following encryption standards should be used to ensure strong security for the VPN connection?

A. DES
B. RC4
C. AES
D. SHA-1

Explanation: The correct answer is C. AES (Advanced Encryption Standard) is recommended for ensuring strong security for VPN connections due to its robust encryption capabilities, making it a suitable choice for securing the remote access to the corporate network.

23. You are tasked with securing data at rest on a storage device. Which of the following encryption standards would be the most appropriate for this purpose?

A. Blowfish
B. Twofish
C. RSA
D. AES-XTS

Explanation: The correct answer is D. AES-XTS (Advanced Encryption Standard-XTS) is specifically designed for securing data at rest on storage devices, providing strong protection against unauthorized access to the stored data, making it the most appropriate choice for this purpose.

24. A company is planning to implement a new encryption solution for its sensitive data. The security team wants to ensure that the chosen solution complies with the Federal Information Processing Standards (FIPS) 140. Which of the following encryption standards should the team consider to ensure FIPS 140 compliance?

A. AES
B. DES
C. RSA
D. MD5

Correct Answer: A. Explanation: The correct answer is AES (Advanced Encryption Standard). FIPS 140-2, a U.S. government security standard, requires the use of approved cryptographic algorithms, and AES is one of the approved algorithms under FIPS 140-2.

25. A new employee has just joined your company. During the onboarding process, they are asked to provide their personal email address and password for setting up their work email. What should you do?

A. Proceed with setting up their work email using the provided credentials.
B. Inform the new employee that company policy prohibits sharing personal email credentials.
C. Set up the work email using temporary credentials and inform the new employee to change the password after the setup.
D. Report the incident to the HR department for further action.

Correct Answer: B. Explanation: It is important to adhere to company policies and security best practices. Sharing personal email credentials is a violation of security policies and should not be allowed during the onboarding process.

26. You are reviewing the playbook procedures for responding to a potential security incident. A team member suggests immediately shutting down the affected system to contain the threat. What should you do?

A) Agree and proceed with shutting down the system.
B) Disagree and explain that shutting down the system may hinder forensic analysis.
C) Escalate the decision to the security manager.
D) Ignore the suggestion and continue with the current course of action.

Explanation: The correct answer is B. Disagree and explain that shutting down the system may hinder forensic analysis. In the context of incident response, it is important to preserve evidence for forensic investigation. Shutting down the system may result in the loss of volatile data, making it difficult to determine the cause and extent of the incident.

27. A company is planning to expand its operations to a European country and needs to comply with the General Data Protection Regulation (GDPR). Which of the following principles is a key aspect of GDPR that the company must consider?

    A) Data minimization
    B) Data obfuscation
    C) Data repudiation
    D) Data proliferation

Correct Answer: A) Data minimization. Explanation: GDPR emphasizes the principle of data minimization, which requires organizations to limit the collection and storage of personal data to what is directly relevant and necessary for a specific purpose.

28. An organization is subject to the Health Insurance Portability and Accountability Act (HIPAA) and needs to ensure the secure disposal of electronic protected health information (ePHI). Which of the following methods should the organization use for secure ePHI disposal?

    A) Overwriting data with zeros once
    B) Degaussing magnetic media
    C) Physical destruction of storage media
    D) Repartitioning hard drives

Correct Answer: C) Physical destruction of storage media
Explanation: HIPAA requires that ePHI be securely disposed of, and physical destruction of storage media, such as shredding or incineration, is one of the recommended methods for ensuring data security.

29. A software development company is preparing to release a new application that will process credit card transactions. Which of the following standards should the company adhere to in order to ensure the security of credit card data?

   A) ISO/IEC 27001
   B) PCI DSS
   C) NIST SP 800-53
   D) FISMA

Correct Answer: B) PCI DSS
Explanation: The Payment Card Industry Data Security Standard (PCI DSS) is specifically designed to enhance payment card data security and is applicable to organizations that handle credit card transactions.

30. A company's security policy states that all security incidents must be reported to the appropriate authorities. Which legal concept does this policy support?

   A) Due process
   B) Due care
   C) Due diligence
   D) Chain of custody

Correct answer: C) Due diligence. Explanation: Due diligence requires organizations to take reasonable steps to prevent and address security incidents. Reporting incidents to the appropriate authorities is a key aspect of fulfilling this legal obligation.

31. A company is implementing a new biometric access control system. Which of the following legal considerations should be addressed first?

   A) GDPR compliance
   B) Employee monitoring laws
   C) Data retention policies
   D) Intellectual property rights

Correct answer: B) Employee monitoring laws. Explanation: When implementing biometric systems, it's crucial to consider and comply with laws related to employee monitoring to ensure the system's legality and the protection of employee rights.

32. You are a security analyst at a large corporation. You discover that an employee has been using company resources to access personal email and social media accounts. What legal concept is being violated?

A) Due care
B) Acceptable use
C) Least privilege
D) Need to know

Correct answer: B) Acceptable use. Explanation: Acceptable use policies define the permitted uses of company resources. Violating these policies can have legal implications, making it the correct answer in this scenario.

33. An organization is planning to store sensitive customer data in a cloud environment. Which of the following legal requirements should be given the highest priority?

A) HIPAA
B) PCI DSS
C) FERPA
D) GDPR

Correct answer: D) GDPR. Explanation: GDPR (General Data Protection Regulation) sets strict guidelines for the processing of personal data. Given the sensitivity of the customer data, ensuring GDPR compliance is of utmost importance.

34. You work at a university and handle student records. A parent calls and requests access to their child's academic records. How should you respond to this request?

A) Provide the parent with access to the records without the student's consent.
B) Request written consent from the student before providing access to the records.
C) Deny the request, as FERPA does not allow access to parents.
D) Ask the parent to provide their own academic records first.

Explanation: The correct answer is B. FERPA gives students over 18 years of age, or attending a postsecondary institution, the right to consent to the disclosure of their educational records. Written consent from the student is required before providing access to the records to a third party, including parents.

35. A company is planning to implement a new cloud-based storage solution for its sensitive data. Which of the following industry considerations should be given the HIGHEST priority?

A. Regulatory compliance
B. Cost-effectiveness
C. Data accessibility
D. Vendor reputation

Correct answer: A. Regulatory compliance. Explanation: When dealing with sensitive data, regulatory compliance should be the highest priority. Failure to comply with industry regulations can lead to legal consequences and data breaches. Cost-effectiveness, data accessibility, and vendor reputation are important but should be secondary to regulatory compliance.

36. A manufacturing firm is considering outsourcing its IT support to a third-party vendor. Which of the following industry considerations is the MOST critical in this scenario?

A. Service-level agreements (SLAs)
B. Cost savings
C. Technical expertise
D. Data sovereignty

Correct answer: D. Data sovereignty. Explanation: In the context of outsourcing IT support, data sovereignty is the most critical consideration. It ensures that the company's data is subject to the laws and regulations of the country in which it is located. While SLAs, cost savings, and technical expertise are important, data sovereignty takes precedence to protect the company's sensitive information.

37. A company with multiple regional offices is planning to implement a new security policy. The policy should account for local regulations and laws related to data protection. Which of the following concepts does this policy primarily address?

A) Least privilege
B) Privacy
C) Data encryption
D) Network segmentation

Correct answer: B) Privacy

Explanation: The scenario describes the need to consider local regulations and laws related to data protection, which falls under the domain of privacy. Implementing a security policy that aligns with local privacy regulations is crucial for legal compliance and data protection.

38. You are a security analyst for a multinational company. The company is planning to expand its operations to a country known for state-sponsored cyber-attacks. Which of the following national considerations should be the primary focus for the company's security strategy?

   A. Legal and regulatory compliance
   B. Geopolitical alliances
   C. Cultural norms
   D. Language barriers

Correct answer: A. Legal and regulatory compliance
Explanation: When expanding operations to a country with a history of state-sponsored cyber-attacks, legal and regulatory compliance should be the primary focus to ensure that the company's security strategy aligns with the local laws and regulations related to cybersecurity.

39. A government contractor is implementing a new system that will store sensitive national security information. Which of the following national considerations is the MOST important for the contractor to address?

   A. Export restrictions
   B. Data sovereignty
   C. Intellectual property rights
   D. Import tariffs

Correct answer: B. Data sovereignty. Explanation: When storing sensitive national security information, data sovereignty is the most important consideration as it ensures that the data is subject to the laws and governance of the country in which it is located, which is crucial for national security purposes.

40. An organization is planning to establish a presence in a country with strict government control over internet access and content. Which of the following national considerations should the organization prioritize when developing its cybersecurity measures?

    A. Privacy laws
    B. Internet censorship
    C. Trade agreements
    D. Currency exchange rates

Correct answer: B. Internet censorship. Explanation: In a country with strict government control over internet access and content, prioritizing measures to address internet censorship is crucial for ensuring that the organization can maintain secure and unrestricted access to essential online resources.

41. A company is considering outsourcing its software development to a country known for intellectual property theft. Which of the following national considerations should be the company's primary concern when evaluating this decision?

    A. Cyber insurance policies
    B. Economic sanctions
    C. Export controls
    D. Intellectual property laws

Correct answer: D. Intellectual property laws. Explanation: When considering outsourcing to a country known for intellectual property theft, the company's primary concern should be the strength and enforcement of intellectual property laws in that country to protect its proprietary software and assets.

42. You are a security analyst for a multinational company. The company is planning to expand its operations to a country with strict data privacy laws. Which of the following should be the PRIMARY consideration when planning the expansion?

A) Implementing encryption for data at rest and in transit
B) Conducting a privacy impact assessment
C) Ensuring compliance with local labor laws
D) Setting up a local security operations center (SOC)

Correct Answer: B. Explanation: When expanding to a country with strict data privacy laws, conducting a privacy impact assessment is crucial to understand and mitigate the potential impact on the company's data handling practices. This assessment will help identify any necessary adjustments to ensure compliance with the local regulations.

43. An organization with a presence in multiple countries is planning to implement a bring your own device (BYOD) policy. Which of the following should be the FIRST step in ensuring the security of the BYOD environment?

A) Implementing containerization for corporate data
B) Developing a comprehensive acceptable use policy (AUP)
C) Conducting a risk assessment for each geographical location
D) Establishing secure remote access solutions

Correct Answer: C. Explanation: Before implementing a BYOD policy, conducting a risk assessment for each geographical location is essential to understand the specific security and compliance challenges posed by the diverse regulatory environments in which the organization operates.

44. You are responsible for monitoring network traffic for your organization. You notice a significant increase in outbound traffic from a specific workstation late at night. What is the most likely cause of this activity?

A) Routine system updates
B) Malware exfiltrating data
C) Scheduled backup process
D) User streaming video

Correct Answer: B. Explanation: A significant increase in outbound traffic late at night from a specific workstation is a common indicator of a potential malware exfiltrating data. Malware often attempts to send stolen data to external servers during off-peak hours to avoid detection.

45. Which of the following best describes the role of a board of directors in an organization's governance structure?

A) Overseeing day-to-day operations
B) Setting the organization's strategic direction
C) Implementing security protocols
D) Managing employee schedules

Explanation: The correct answer is B. Boards of directors are responsible for setting the organization's strategic direction, making important decisions, and overseeing the management of the company. They are not involved in day-to-day operations, implementing security protocols, or managing employee schedules.

46. What is the primary responsibility of an advisory board in a governance structure?

A) Making operational decisions
B) Providing strategic advice
C) Enforcing company policies
D) Managing financial accounts

Explanation: The correct answer is B. An advisory board provides strategic advice and guidance to the organization. They are not involved in making operational decisions, enforcing company policies, or managing financial accounts.

47. You are a security administrator in a large organization. The company is planning to form a committee to oversee the implementation of a new security policy. Which of the following is the primary purpose of this committee?

A) To make all security-related decisions
B) To provide oversight and guidance
C) To delegate security responsibilities
D) To enforce security policies

Correct answer: B. Explanation: The primary purpose of the committee is to provide oversight and guidance, ensuring that the security policy is effectively implemented and followed by the organization. The committee is not responsible for making all security-related decisions, delegating security responsibilities, or enforcing security policies.

48. A small town is planning to implement a new system for managing public services, including water, electricity, and waste management. Which of the following government entities would be primarily responsible for overseeing this initiative?

A. Department of Homeland Security
B. Environmental Protection Agency
C. Department of Public Works
D. Federal Trade Commission

Correct Answer: C. Department of Public Works. Explanation: The Department of Public Works is typically responsible for the planning, construction, and maintenance of public infrastructure, making it the most relevant government entity for overseeing the implementation of a system for managing public services in a town.

49. A company has recently experienced a data breach. The IT team is reviewing the incident response process. In which governance structure is the decision-making authority typically distributed across various departments or business units?

A. Centralized
B. Decentralized
C. Hybrid
D. None of the above

Correct Answer: B. Decentralized. In a decentralized governance structure, decision-making authority is distributed across various departments or business units. This allows for quicker decision-making and greater flexibility in responding to incidents, making it an effective approach for incident response processes.

50. A multinational corporation is planning to implement a new security policy that will apply to all its subsidiaries and regional offices. In which governance structure would this policy be most effectively enforced from a single central location?

A. Centralized
B. Decentralized
C. Federated
D. None of the above

Correct Answer: A. Centralized. In a centralized governance structure, policies and decision-making authority are concentrated at a single central location. This ensures consistency and uniformity in policy enforcement across the organization, making it the most effective approach for implementing a new security policy in a multinational corporation.

51. You are a data owner in a large organization. You receive a request from a department manager to provide access to sensitive customer data for a new analytics project. What is your most appropriate course of action?

A) Immediately grant the access request to facilitate the project's progress.
B) Request a written explanation of the business need and consult with the relevant stakeholders before making a decision.
C) Deny the request without further consideration to avoid potential data exposure.
D) Delegate the decision to the IT department to handle without your involvement.

Explanation: The correct answer is B. As a data owner, it is essential to ensure that access to sensitive data is based on a legitimate business need and is in line with organizational policies and regulations. Consulting with stakeholders and evaluating the business justification are crucial steps in maintaining data security and integrity.

52. You are assessing the data protection measures of a company. You discover that the data controller is responsible for determining the purposes and means of processing personal data. Which of the following best describes the role of a data controller?

A) Implements technical measures to secure data
B) Determines how and why personal data is processed
C) Manages data storage and retrieval
D) Ensures compliance with data subject requests

Correct Answer: B. Explanation: The data controller is responsible for determining how and why personal data is processed, making option B the correct choice.

53. A company is evaluating a cloud service provider for storing and processing sensitive customer data. Which of the following should the company consider to ensure compliance with data protection regulations?

A. The physical location of the data centers
B. The number of virtual machines in the cloud environment
C. The brand of the servers used by the cloud provider
D. The color of the server racks in the data centers

Correct Answer: A. Explanation: Data protection regulations often require that sensitive data be stored and processed within specific jurisdictions. Therefore, the physical location of the data centers is a critical factor in ensuring compliance with these regulations.

54. A company has recently implemented a new data governance framework. The IT team is in the process of identifying data custodians for different types of data. Who among the following individuals is most likely to be assigned as a data custodian?

A. Chief Executive Officer (CEO)
B. Database Administrator (DBA)
C. Human Resources Manager
D. Marketing Manager

Correct Answer: B. Explanation: The correct answer is the Database Administrator (DBA). A data custodian is responsible for the storage, maintenance, and protection of the data. The DBA typically has the technical expertise and access rights to fulfill this role effectively.

55. In a large financial organization, a new regulation requires the appointment of data stewards for different business units. Who among the following individuals is most likely to be appointed as a data steward?

A. Chief Financial Officer (CFO)
B. Business Analyst
C. Customer Service Representative
D. Software Developer

Correct Answer: B. Explanation: The correct answer is the Business Analyst. Data stewards are responsible for defining and implementing data standards within their respective business units. Business Analysts often have a deep understanding of the data and its usage within their areas, making them suitable for this role.

56. You are conducting a risk assessment for your organization's network. Which of the following is an example of a vulnerability?

A) Outdated antivirus software
B) Strong firewall configuration
C) Regular security training for employees
D) Encrypted data transmission

Correct Answer: A. Explanation: An outdated antivirus software is a vulnerability as it can be exploited by malware and other threats. Vulnerabilities are weaknesses in a system that can be exploited to compromise the security of the system.

57. You are a security analyst in a large organization. The IT department is planning to roll out a new software system to all employees. However, due to time constraints, a formal risk assessment cannot be conducted. What type of risk assessment is being performed in this scenario?

A) Qualitative risk assessment
B) Quantitative risk assessment
C) Ad hoc risk assessment
D) Continuous risk assessment

Correct Answer: C) Ad hoc risk assessment. Explanation: In this scenario, the risk assessment is being performed informally and on an as-needed basis due to time constraints, which aligns with the definition of ad hoc risk assessment. This type of assessment is conducted in response to specific circumstances or needs, without following a formal process or methodology.

58. You are performing a recurring risk assessment for your organization. Which of the following best describes the purpose of this assessment?

A) To identify new security threats
B) To evaluate the effectiveness of existing security controls
C) To create a baseline for security performance
D) To calculate the return on security investment

Correct Answer: B. Explanation: The purpose of a recurring risk assessment is to evaluate the effectiveness of existing security controls. This helps in identifying any weaknesses or areas that need improvement in the organization's security posture.

59. During a recurring risk assessment, you discover that a software patch for a critical vulnerability has not been applied to several systems. What should be your immediate next step?

A) Apply the patch to the systems
B) Document the finding and report it to the IT department
C) Ignore the issue as it is not currently being exploited
D) Conduct a cost-benefit analysis of applying the patch

Correct Answer: B. Explanation: In this scenario, the immediate next step should be to document the finding and report it to the IT department. This is essential for ensuring that the necessary actions are taken to address the vulnerability and improve the security posture.

60. When conducting a one-time risk assessment for a network infrastructure upgrade, which of the following should be considered a vulnerability?

A) Redundant power supply
B) Encrypted data transmission
C) Outdated firmware
D) Access control list (ACL)

Correct Answer: C. Explanation: Outdated firmware is a vulnerability as it can be exploited by attackers to compromise the network security.

61. During a one-time risk assessment for a data center relocation, which of the following is an example of a single loss expectancy (SLE) calculation?

A) Assessing the cost of implementing new security controls
B) Estimating the potential financial loss from a server outage
C) Evaluating the impact of regulatory compliance on the project
D) Analyzing the performance of network redundancy measures

Correct Answer: B. Explanation: Estimating the potential financial loss from a server outage is an example of calculating the single loss expectancy (SLE) as part of risk assessment.

62. You are implementing a continuous risk assessment process in your organization. Which of the following best describes the primary goal of continuous risk assessment?

A) Conducting annual risk evaluations
B) Identifying new risks as they emerge
C) Minimizing all potential risks
D) Focusing only on technical vulnerabilities

Explanation: The correct answer is B. Continuous risk assessment aims to identify new risks as they emerge, allowing organizations to proactively address evolving threats and vulnerabilities.

63. As part of continuous risk assessment, which of the following is a key benefit of using automated tools?

A) Reduced need for skilled personnel
B) Limited scope of risk coverage
C) Real-time risk identification
D) Inflexibility in adapting to new threats

Explanation: The correct answer is C. Automated tools enable real-time risk identification, providing organizations with timely insights into their security posture.

64. You are performing a qualitative risk analysis for your organization. Which of the following best describes the purpose of this process?

A) To assign a dollar value to each risk
B) To prioritize risks based on their potential impact and likelihood
C) To identify specific vulnerabilities in the organization's systems
D) To create a detailed response plan for each risk

Correct Answer: B. Explanation: The purpose of qualitative risk analysis is to prioritize risks based on their potential impact and likelihood. This helps the organization focus on addressing the most significant risks first.

65. You are performing a quantitative risk analysis for your organization. Which of the following is a key input to this process?

A) Asset valuation
B) Vulnerability assessment
C) Qualitative risk assessment
D) Threat modeling

Correct answer: A) Asset valuation. Explanation: Asset valuation is a key input to quantitative risk analysis as it provides the monetary value of the assets at risk, which is essential for calculating potential loss exposure and risk exposure. The other options are important in the risk analysis process but are not direct inputs to quantitative risk analysis.

66. You are assessing the potential impact of a security breach on your organization's server. The server has an asset value of $50,000 and there is a 10% chance of a security breach occurring in the next year. If a breach occurs, the potential loss is estimated to be $30,000. What is the Single Loss Expectancy (SLE) for this security breach?

   A) $5,000
   B) $15,000
   C) $30,000
   D) $50,000

Correct Answer: B) $15,000. Explanation: The Single Loss Expectancy (SLE) is calculated by multiplying the asset value by the annualized rate of occurrence and the loss magnitude. In this scenario, SLE = $50,000 (asset value) * 0.10 (annualized rate of occurrence) * $30,000 (loss magnitude) = $15,000.

67. You are assessing the potential impact of a security breach on your organization. The asset in question has a value of $100,000, and the exposure factor is determined to be 40%. The annualized rate of occurrence of the threat is 0.05. What is the Annualized Loss Expectancy (ALE) for this asset?

   A) $2,000
   B) $4,000
   C) $8,000
   D) $20,000

Correct Answer: B) $4,000
Explanation: ALE is calculated by multiplying the asset value by the exposure factor and the annualized rate of occurrence. In this case, ALE = $100,000 * 40% * 0.05 = $4,000.

68. You are assessing the risk of a potential security threat. After conducting a thorough analysis, you determine that the ARO for this threat is 0.05. What does this value indicate?

   A) The threat is likely to occur once every 5 years.
   B) The threat is likely to occur 5 times a year.
   C) The threat is unlikely to occur.
   D) The threat is certain to occur.

Explanation:
The correct answer is A. ARO represents the estimated frequency with which a specific threat is expected to occur. A value of 0.05 indicates that the threat is likely to occur once every 5 years.

69. You are performing a probability risk analysis for a new software project. The team has identified a potential risk with a 20% probability of occurring. Which of the following best describes this probability?

A) Low
B) Medium
C) High
D) Critical

Correct Answer: A) Low. Explanation: A 20% probability of occurrence is considered low in risk analysis. It indicates that the risk is not highly likely to occur, and mitigations may be less urgent compared to risks with higher probabilities.

70. You are performing a Likelihood Risk analysis for a new software implementation project. Which of the following factors should you consider to assess the likelihood of a security breach?

A) The number of security controls in place
B) The geographical location of the project team
C) The brand reputation of the software vendor
D) The programming language used for the software

Correct Answer: A. Explanation: When assessing the likelihood of a security breach, the number of security controls in place is a critical factor. This includes measures such as access controls, encryption, and monitoring systems, which directly impact the probability of a security incident.

71. During a Likelihood Risk analysis, which of the following best describes how the annualized loss expectancy (ALE) is calculated?

A) Multiplying the asset value by the exposure factor
B) Adding the single loss expectancy to the annual loss frequency
C) Dividing the asset value by the exposure factor
D) Subtracting the safeguard value from the asset value

Correct Answer: B. Explanation: The annualized loss expectancy (ALE) is calculated by adding the single loss expectancy (SLE) to the annual loss frequency (ALF). This provides a measure of the expected loss from a specific risk over the course of a year.

72. A company is assessing the impact of a potential security breach. If the breach were to occur, and it is estimated that 70% of the data would be exposed, what is the exposure factor?

A) 30%
B) 70%
C) 100%
D) 50%

Correct answer is B) 70%. Explanation: The exposure factor is the percentage of data that is expected to be compromised if a security breach occurs. In this scenario, if 70% of the data would be exposed, the exposure factor is 70%. Therefore, the correct answer is B) 70%.

73. You are performing an impact risk analysis for a company's financial system. Which of the following best describes the impact if the system is unavailable for 24 hours?

A) Low
B) Medium
C) High
D) Critical

Correct Answer: C) High. Explanation: The unavailability of the financial system for 24 hours would have a high impact on the company's operations, potentially leading to significant financial losses and disruption of business activities.

74. During a risk analysis, it is determined that the loss of customer data could result in legal implications and damage to the company's reputation. What type of impact is this?

A) Financial
B) Reputational
C) Operational
D) Compliance

Correct Answer: B) Reputational. Explanation: The loss of customer data leading to legal implications and damage to the company's reputation represents a reputational impact, as it affects how the company is perceived by its customers and the public.

75. You are conducting a risk assessment for your organization. Which of the following would be considered a Key Risk Indicator (KRI) for a potential cyber attack?

A) Number of security training sessions conducted
B) Increase in failed login attempts
C) Employee satisfaction survey results
D) Revenue generated in the last quarter

Correct Answer: B. Explanation: An increase in failed login attempts is a KRI for a potential cyber attack as it indicates a higher risk of unauthorized access attempts, which is a common precursor to a cyber attack.

76. As part of your organization's risk management process, which of the following would be the most relevant Key Risk Indicator (KRI) for identifying a potential data breach?

A) Server uptime percentage
B) Number of security patches applied
C) Employee turnover rate
D) Customer satisfaction ratings

Correct Answer: B. Explanation: The number of security patches applied is a KRI for identifying a potential data breach as unpatched systems are more vulnerable to security threats, making this indicator relevant for risk assessment.

77. Which of the following best describes a risk owner?

A) The individual or group responsible for the day-to-day implementation and maintenance of risk management processes.
B) The person or entity that has the authority to manage and accept risks on behalf of the organization.
C) The individual who identifies potential risks within an organization.
D) The team in charge of developing risk mitigation strategies.

Explanation: The correct answer is B. The risk owner is the person or entity that has the authority to manage and accept risks on behalf of the organization. This individual or group is ultimately accountable for the risk and has the responsibility to ensure that it is properly managed and mitigated.

78. You are a security analyst for a large financial institution. The organization is considering implementing a new online banking platform. The project team has identified potential risks associated with the new platform. What should be the primary consideration when determining the risk threshold for this project?

A) The cost of implementing security controls
B) The potential impact of a security breach on customer data
C) The technical specifications of the online banking platform
D) The project timeline and budget

Correct Answer: B. Explanation: When determining the risk threshold for a project, the potential impact of a security breach on customer data should be the primary consideration. This aligns with the organization's goal of protecting sensitive information and maintaining customer trust.

79. You are the security administrator for a large financial institution. The board of directors is discussing the organization's risk tolerance. Which of the following best defines risk tolerance in this context?

A) The level of risk that the organization is willing to accept.
B) The likelihood of a security breach occurring.
C) The cost of implementing security controls.
D) The impact of a security incident on the organization's reputation.

Correct Answer: A. Explanation: Risk tolerance refers to the level of risk that an organization is willing to accept. It is an important factor in determining the appropriate security controls and risk management strategies.

80. You are a security analyst for a large financial institution. The company is considering investing in a new technology that promises to streamline operations but comes with potential security risks. The CEO is known for being open to taking risks to stay ahead of the competition. This approach to risk is an example of:

A) High risk aversion
B) Expansionary risk tolerance
C) Risk neutrality
D) Risk acceptance

Correct Answer: B. Explanation: Expansionary risk tolerance is characterized by a willingness to take on higher levels of risk in pursuit of potential rewards. In this scenario, the CEO's openness to the potential security risks associated with the new technology aligns with expansionary risk tolerance.

81. You are a security analyst at a financial institution known for its conservative approach to risk. A new software update is available for the institution's core banking system, which includes critical security patches. However, the update has not been extensively tested. What is the most appropriate action to take?

A) Immediately apply the update to mitigate potential security vulnerabilities.
B) Delay the update until it undergoes thorough testing to ensure minimal disruption.
C) Apply the update to a small subset of systems to gauge its impact before full deployment.
D) Ignore the update to avoid any potential negative impact on the banking system.

Explanation: The correct answer is B. In a conservative risk tolerance environment, it is essential to prioritize stability and minimize disruption. Delaying the update until it undergoes thorough testing aligns with this approach, ensuring that the institution's critical systems remain stable and secure.

82. You are a security analyst at a financial institution with a neutral risk tolerance. A new software update is available for the institution's online banking platform. Which of the following actions is most appropriate in this scenario?

A) Immediately install the update to ensure the latest features are available.
B) Conduct thorough testing of the update in a controlled environment before deploying it to the production system.
C) Delay the update indefinitely to avoid potential disruptions to the online banking services.
D) Install the update during peak hours to minimize the impact on customer transactions.

Explanation: The correct answer is B. In a neutral risk tolerance environment, it's important to balance the need for security with the potential impact of changes. Thorough testing in a controlled environment aligns with this approach, as it helps mitigate the risk of disrupting critical services.

83. You are a security analyst at a financial institution. The company is considering transferring the risk of a potential cyber attack to a third-party insurance provider. Which of the following best describes the concept of risk transfer in this scenario?

A) Shifting the financial burden of a potential loss to an insurance company
B) Eliminating the possibility of a cyber attack
C) Accepting the risk without any mitigation measures
D) Increasing the likelihood of a successful cyber attack

Explanation: The correct answer is A) Shifting the financial burden of a potential loss to an insurance company. Risk transfer involves transferring the financial consequences of a risk to another party, such as an insurance company. This allows the organization to mitigate the impact of a potential loss by paying premiums to the insurance provider in exchange for coverage in the event of a cyber attack.

84. You are the security administrator for a large e-commerce company. After conducting a risk assessment, you identify a potential risk related to a new online payment system. The risk assessment indicates that the cost of implementing additional security measures outweighs the potential loss from a security breach. What risk management strategy are you employing?

A. Risk avoidance
B. Risk transference
C. Risk acceptance
D. Risk mitigation

Correct Answer: C. Explanation: In this scenario, the organization has decided to accept the risk associated with the new online payment system, as the cost of implementing additional security measures is higher than the potential loss from a security breach. This is an example of risk acceptance, where the organization acknowledges the risk and decides not to take any further action to address it.

85. You are a project manager for a software development project. During the risk assessment phase, it is identified that a critical component of the system has a high probability of failure due to a known software bug. The development team suggests bypassing the testing phase for this component to meet the project deadline. What is the most appropriate course of action?

A. Proceed with the testing phase as planned and address the software bug.
B. Bypass the testing phase for the critical component to meet the project deadline.
C. Accept the risk of potential failure and proceed with the project as scheduled.
D. Inform the stakeholders about the software bug and seek approval to extend the project deadline.

Explanation: The correct answer is A. Proceeding with the testing phase as planned and addressing the software bug is the most appropriate course of action. Bypassing the testing phase (option B) and accepting the risk of potential failure (option C) are not recommended as they can lead to serious consequences. Informing the stakeholders about the software bug and seeking approval to extend the project deadline (option D) is important, but addressing the issue through proper testing is crucial to mitigate the risk.

86. A company is considering a new software that is known to have some security vulnerabilities. The IT team has assessed the risks and determined that the benefits of the software outweigh the potential security risks. What risk management strategy are they employing?

A. Risk avoidance
B. Risk transference
C. Risk acceptance
D. Risk mitigation

Correct Answer: C. Risk acceptance. Explanation: In this scenario, the company is aware of the security risks associated with the software but has chosen to accept these risks due to the benefits it offers. Risk acceptance involves acknowledging the potential risks and deciding to proceed without taking further action to reduce them.

87. A company is considering implementing a new cloud-based storage solution. The solution offers high scalability and accessibility but is known to have potential security vulnerabilities. The company's risk management strategy focuses on maximizing opportunities. Which of the following risk responses is the company pursuing?

A) Accepting risk
B) Avoiding risk
C) Transferring risk
D) Mitigating risk

Explanation: The correct answer is A) Accepting risk. By focusing on maximizing opportunities, the company is willing to accept the potential security vulnerabilities associated with the cloud-based storage solution, as it values the benefits of scalability and accessibility. This aligns with the concept of accepting risk, where an organization acknowledges the potential impact of a risk and decides to deal with it as part of its strategy.

88. An organization has identified a potential risk of data breaches due to outdated security measures. To mitigate this risk, they decide to implement a new firewall and update their intrusion detection system. Which risk mitigation strategy is being used?

A) Risk acceptance
B) Risk avoidance
C) Risk transference
D) Risk reduction

Correct answer: D) Risk reduction. Explanation: The organization is reducing the risk of data breaches by implementing new security measures, such as a firewall and updated intrusion detection system, to minimize the impact of potential security incidents

89. You are a security analyst at a large financial institution. You have been tasked with preparing a risk report for the board of directors. Which of the following should be included in the report to best communicate the potential impact of identified risks?

A) Technical vulnerability details
B) Business impact analysis
C) Security control effectiveness
D) Incident response procedures

Correct Answer: B. Explanation: Business impact analysis is essential for communicating the potential impact of identified risks to the board of directors. It focuses on the potential financial, operational, and reputational consequences of the risks, which is crucial for business decision-making.

90. A security analyst is preparing a risk report for their organization's management. Which of the following should the analyst include in the report?

A. A list of all known software vulnerabilities
B. An assessment of the organization's overall risk posture
C. A detailed explanation of the organization's encryption methods
D. A list of all employees who have access to sensitive data

Correct Answer: B. Explanation: Risk reporting is about providing management with an overview of the organization's risk posture, which includes identifying, assessing, and prioritizing risks. While other options may be relevant in specific contexts, the most appropriate option for a risk report is an assessment of the organization's overall risk posture.

91. What is the primary goal of a Business Impact Analysis (BIA)?

A. Identify critical IT systems
B. Prioritize IT disaster recovery efforts
C. Assess the feasibility of implementing a disaster recovery plan
D. Evaluate the effectiveness of existing disaster recovery plans

Correct Answer: B. Prioritize IT disaster recovery efforts
Explanation: The primary goal of a BIA is to determine the potential impacts of a disaster on a company's operations and prioritize the recovery of critical business processes and IT systems.

92. Which of the following is NOT a component of a Business Impact Analysis (BIA)?

A. Identification of critical business processes
B. Determination of the maximum tolerable downtime (MTD)
C. Assessment of the financial impact of a disaster
D. Evaluation of employee training and preparedness

Correct Answer: D. Explanation: While employee training and preparedness are important aspects of disaster recovery planning, they are not directly components of a BIA, which focuses on identifying critical processes and determining the necessary recovery time objectives (RTO) and recovery point objectives (RPO).

93. A company is reviewing its Recovery Time Objective (RTO) for its email system. The company has determined that it can afford to be without email for up to 8 hours without significant damage. The company should:

A. Set an RTO of 8 hours for its email system.
B. Set an RTO of 4 hours for its email system.
C. Set an RTO of 12 hours for its email system.
D. Set an RTO of 2 hours for its email system.

Answer: A. Explanation: RTO is the maximum amount of time that a business can afford to be without a particular system or application before significant damage occurs. In this scenario, the company has determined that it can afford to be without email for up to 8 hours without significant damage. Therefore, the company should set an RTO of 8 hours for its email system to reflect this tolerance for downtime.

94. A company has a recovery point objective of 4 hours and a recovery time objective of 6 hours. The company experiences a data loss incident at 8 AM. How much data will the company lose?

A. 0 hours
B. 4 hours
C. 6 hours
D. 8 hours

Answer: B. Explanation: The recovery point objective (RPO) is the maximum age of the data that can be lost after a recovery from a backup is initiated. In this case, the RPO is 4 hours. Since the company experiences a data loss incident at 8 AM and the recovery time objective (RTO) is 6 hours, the company will lose 4 hours of data, which is the difference between the RPO and the RTO.

95. A network administrator is evaluating the MTTR of a company's incident response process. The administrator identifies the following data for the past year:
- Incidents: 10
- Total downtime: 8 hours

What is the MTTR in this case?
A. 48 minutes
B. 50 minutes
C. 40 minutes
D. 60 minutes

Answer: A. Explanation: To calculate MTTR, divide the total downtime by the number of incidents. In this case, 8 hours of downtime divided by 10 incidents equals 48 minutes.

96. A network administrator is evaluating the reliability of a network device. Which of the following is NOT a component of MTBF?

  A. The total number of hours the device is operational

  B. The total number of hours the device is non-operational

  C. The total number of hours the device is in sleep mode

  D. The total number of hours the device is in standby mode

Correct Answer: B. Explanation: MTBF is calculated by dividing the total number of operational hours by the total number of failures. It does not consider the time the device is non-operational, such as during maintenance or upgrades.

97. A company wants to assess the security of a vendor that provides cloud-based storage solutions. Which of the following assessment methods should the company consider?

  A. Vulnerability scanning

  B. Penetration testing

  C. Request for Information (RFI)

  D. Request for Proposal (RFP)

Answer: A. Vulnerability scanning

Explanation: Vulnerability scanning is an assessment method that identifies vulnerabilities in a system, application, or network. In the context of assessing a vendor's security, a vulnerability scan can help the company identify potential security weaknesses in the vendor's cloud-based storage solutions before they are exploited by attackers.

98. A penetration tester is performing a web application penetration test on a target system. They identify a vulnerability that allows them to inject malicious SQL code into a database. Which type of vulnerability is this?

      A. Cross-site Scripting (XSS)
      B. SQL Injection
      C. Command Injection
      D. Buffer Overflow

Answer: B. SQL Injection. SQL injection is a technique used to exploit vulnerabilities in a web application's database layer by injecting malicious SQL code. This can lead to unauthorized access, data theft, or corruption of data.

99. Which of the following best describes the purpose of a Right-to-audit clause in a contract?

      A. Allows the vendor to review the client's financial records
      B. Requires the vendor to provide a detailed project plan
      C. Enables the client to verify the vendor's compliance with the contract terms
      D. Mandates the vendor to disclose their source code

Correct Answer: C. Explanation: The Right-to-audit clause is a provision in a contract that allows one party (usually the client) to review and verify the performance, procedures, or records of the other party (usually the vendor) to ensure compliance with the contract terms. This clause helps protect the client's interests by providing a mechanism to monitor the vendor's activities and confirm that they are meeting the agreed-upon requirements.

100. Which of the following is NOT a purpose of internal audit evidence?

    A. To provide a reasonable basis for the auditor's opinion

    B. To detect fraud

    C. To provide management with assurance

    D. To support the financial statements

Correct Answer: B. Explanation: The purpose of internal audit evidence is to provide a reasonable basis for the auditor's opinion, to support the financial statements, and to provide management with assurance. While internal audits can help detect fraud, their primary focus is on providing assurance and evaluating the effectiveness of internal controls.

101. A company has hired an independent auditor to assess their IT security infrastructure. The auditor discovers that the company's wireless network is open and unencrypted. Which of the following recommendations should the auditor make to the company?

    A. Implement a strong encryption protocol

    B. Upgrade the wireless router's firmware

    C. Increase the number of wireless access points

    D. Implement a VPN for remote access

Answer: A. Explanation: The auditor should recommend implementing a strong encryption protocol, such as WPA2 or WPA3, to secure the wireless network and protect sensitive data from unauthorized access.

102. A company wants to ensure that its supply chain is secure and reliable. Which of the following should the company consider during a supply chain analysis audit?
- A. Evaluating the security measures of suppliers and subcontractors
- B. Assessing the company's internal processes and controls
- C. Reviewing the company's financial statements
- D. Analyzing the company's marketing strategies

Answer: A. Explanation: Supply chain analysis audits focus on assessing the security and reliability of a company's suppliers and subcontractors. This includes evaluating the security measures these entities have in place to protect the company's information and assets.

103. Which of the following is NOT a factor to consider when selecting a third-party vendor for risk management?
- A. The vendor's financial stability
- B. The vendor's security and compliance track record
- C. The vendor's location and jurisdiction
- D. The vendor's marketing strategy

Correct Answer: D. Explanation: When selecting a third-party vendor for risk management, it is essential to consider factors such as the vendor's financial stability, security and compliance track record, and location and jurisdiction. However, the vendor's marketing strategy is not a critical factor in determining their suitability for managing risks.

104. What is the primary goal of a third-party risk assessment in the context of vendor selection?

A. To evaluate the vendor's marketing strategy
B. To identify and assess potential risks associated with the vendor
C. To determine the vendor's pricing structure
D. To assess the vendor's customer service quality

Correct Answer: B. Explanation: The primary goal of a third-party risk assessment is to identify and assess potential risks associated with the vendor, such as cybersecurity risks, compliance risks, and financial risks. This process helps organizations determine the level of risk they face by working with a particular vendor and make informed decisions about whether to proceed with the relationship.

105. A company has hired a third-party vendor to manage their payroll system. Identify the potential conflict of interest in this scenario.

A. The third-party vendor has access to sensitive employee data.
B. The company's IT department is responsible for monitoring the third-party vendor's performance.
C. The third-party vendor is also managing the company's CRM system.
D. The company's management is related to the third-party vendor's management.

Correct Answer: A. Explanation: The correct answer is A, as a potential conflict of interest arises when the third-party vendor has access to sensitive employee data. This access could lead to data breaches, unauthorized access, or misuse of sensitive information, which could negatively impact the company and its employees.

106. A company has outsourced its payroll processing to a third-party service provider. Which of the following is the primary concern regarding the Service-Level Agreement (SLA) for this scenario?

A. The third-party provider's employees are not trained in data security.
B. The third-party provider does not have a robust incident response plan.
C. The third-party provider does not have a compliant privacy policy.
D. The third-party provider does not have a plan for disaster recovery.

Correct Answer: A. Explanation: The primary concern regarding the SLA for outsourcing payroll processing is whether the third-party provider's employees are trained in data security. This is because payroll processing involves handling sensitive employee data, such as Social Security numbers, bank account information, and salary details. Ensuring that the third-party provider's employees are trained in data security is crucial to protecting this sensitive information from unauthorized access, loss, or theft.

107. A company has recently entered into a third-party risk management Memorandum of Agreement (MOA) with a service provider. The service provider is responsible for handling sensitive customer data. Which of the following is the primary objective of this MOA?

A. To establish a pricing model for the services provided by the service provider
B. To define the roles and responsibilities of both parties in managing the risk associated with the service provider's operations
C. To outline the service provider's service level agreements (SLAs) for the company
D. To determine the company's liability in case of a data breach involving the service provider

Answer: B. Explanation: The primary objective of a third-party risk management MOA is to establish the roles and responsibilities of both parties in managing the risk associated with the service provider's operations. This includes outlining the controls and processes that the service provider must have in place to protect the company's data and ensuring that the service provider maintains an acceptable level of risk.

108. A company is considering entering into a third-party risk management MOU with a service provider. Which of the following should the company include in the MOU to ensure the service provider follows best security practices?

A. Require the service provider to comply with all applicable laws and regulations.
B. Specify the type of software and hardware to be used by the service provider.
C. Include a clause that allows the company to audit the service provider's security controls.
D. Mandate that the service provider follow the company's internal security policies.

Answer: C. Explanation: Auditing the service provider's security controls allows the company to ensure that the service provider is following best security practices and maintaining an acceptable level of risk. While compliance with laws and regulations (option a) is important, it does not guarantee that the service provider's security practices are adequate. Specifying software and hardware (option b) may be too restrictive and may not address all security concerns. Following the company's internal security policies (option d) may not be practical or appropriate for the service provider's operations.

109. A company is evaluating a third-party service provider to manage their payroll system. The company's security team is concerned about the potential risks associated with sharing sensitive employee data. Which of the following should the company consider including in the MSA to mitigate risks?

A. Require the third-party provider to comply with all applicable data protection regulations.
B. Mandate that the third-party provider's employees undergo background checks.
C. Include a clause that limits the third-party provider's liability in case of a data breach.
D. Specify that the third-party provider is responsible for maintaining the company's cybersecurity standards.

Answer: A. Explanation: Compliance with data protection regulations ensures that the third-party provider adheres to the required security standards, reducing the risk of data breaches and potential legal consequences. While background checks (option b) and cybersecurity standards (option d) are important, they do not directly address the compliance aspect. Limiting the third-party provider's liability (option c) may not be in the best interest of the company, as it could discourage the provider from taking necessary security measures.

110. A company is hiring a third-party vendor to manage their payroll system. Which of the following should be included in the Statement of Work (SOW) to ensure proper risk management?

A. Detailed requirements for the payroll system
B. Vendor's financial stability
C. Employee background check requirements
D. Company's acceptable use policy

Answer: A. Explanation: The Statement of Work (SOW) should include detailed requirements for the payroll system to ensure that the third-party vendor understands the company's expectations and can meet them. This helps to mitigate potential risks associated with the vendor's performance and protect sensitive employee data. While other options may be relevant in certain contexts, they are not directly related to risk management in the SOW.

111. A company is working with a third-party vendor to develop a new software application. Which of the following should be included in the Work Order (WO) to ensure proper risk management?

A. Requirements for data backup and recovery
B. Vendor's security policies and procedures
C. Employee training requirements
D. Company's code of conduct

Answer: B. Vendor's security policies and procedures
Explanation: The Work Order (WO) should include the vendor's security policies and procedures to ensure that the vendor maintains an appropriate level of security throughout the development process. This helps to protect the company's intellectual property and sensitive data from potential security threats. While other options may be relevant in certain contexts, they are not directly related to risk management in the WO.

112. A company is considering entering into a third-party risk management Non-disclosure Agreement (NDA) with a software vendor. Which of the following should the company consider including in the NDA to ensure the protection of its sensitive information?

A. A clause specifying the vendor's security controls and policies
B. A clause requiring the vendor to provide annual security audit reports
C. A clause stating that the vendor will not share the company's information with any subcontractors
D. A clause specifying the vendor's data breach notification procedures

Correct Answer: A. Explanation: In a third-party risk management NDA, it is essential to include a clause specifying the vendor's security controls and policies to ensure the protection of the company's sensitive information. This clause should outline the minimum security standards the vendor must meet, such as encryption, access controls, and incident response plans. By including this clause, the company can better protect its data and minimize the risk of unauthorized access or disclosure.

113. A company has entered into a BPA with a third-party service provider to outsource its payroll processing. The company wants to ensure the security of its employee data. Which of the following should the company include in the BPA to mitigate risks?

A. Limit the number of employees who can access the payroll system
B. Require the third-party provider to adhere to the company's security policies and standards
C. Implement a backup plan to store payroll data in case of a security breach
D. Encrypt all payroll data before transmitting it to the third-party provider

Answer: B. Explanation: In a BPA, it is crucial to include provisions that ensure the third-party provider follows the same security policies and standards as the company. This helps protect sensitive data and prevent security breaches. While options a, c, and d are also important security measures, they should be considered in addition to, rather than instead of, requiring the third-party provider to adhere to the company's security policies and standards.

114. A company has implemented a third-party risk management program to monitor vendors. Which of the following should be the primary objective of this program?

A. Ensuring the lowest possible cost of goods and services from vendors
B. Establishing and maintaining an inventory of all vendors and their risk profiles
C. Minimizing the number of vendors used by the company
D. Ensuring the highest level of security and compliance with regulations

Correct Answer: B. Explanation: The primary objective of a third-party risk management program should be to establish and maintain an inventory of all vendors and their risk profiles. This includes assessing the security and compliance posture of each vendor, monitoring their performance, and mitigating risks associated with their services.

115. A company is evaluating a third-party vendor to handle their data backup and recovery services. Which of the following factors should the company consider the most when assessing the vendor's risk?

A. The vendor's pricing structure
B. The vendor's reputation in the industry
C. The vendor's security controls and policies
D. The vendor's location and proximity to the company

Answer: C. Explanation: When assessing a third-party vendor's risk, it is crucial to consider their security controls and policies. This includes evaluating their security standards, compliance with relevant regulations, and the effectiveness of their risk management practices. While factors like pricing, reputation, and location may also be important, the primary concern should be the vendor's ability to protect the company's data and maintain a secure environment.

116. A company wants to establish a third-party risk management program to ensure that all third-party vendors and partners adhere to the same security standards as the company. Which of the following is the MOST important aspect of this program?

A. Defining clear roles and responsibilities for both the company and third parties
B. Implementing a robust incident response plan
C. Conducting regular penetration testing of third-party systems
D. Ensuring compliance with industry-specific regulations

Answer: A. Explanation: Defining clear roles and responsibilities is crucial in a third-party risk management program. It ensures that both the company and third parties understand their obligations and are held accountable for maintaining security standards. This approach minimizes the risk of security breaches due to third-party negligence or mismanagement. While other options, such as incident response plans and penetration testing, are important aspects of a security program, they are not the most critical for third-party risk management.

117. A company is evaluating a third-party vendor for potential collaboration. Which of the following assessment methods would provide the GREATEST level of assurance regarding the vendor's security posture?

A. Reviewing the vendor's security policies and procedures
B. Conducting a questionnaire-based assessment of the vendor's security practices
C. Performing a technical assessment of the vendor's network and systems
D. Relying on the vendor's assertion of compliance with industry standards

Answer: C. Performing a technical assessment of the vendor's network and systems

Explanation: Performing a technical assessment of the vendor's network and systems provides the greatest level of assurance regarding their security posture. This hands-on approach allows the company to identify potential vulnerabilities and validate the effectiveness of the vendor's security controls. While reviewing policies and procedures or conducting a questionnaire-based assessment may provide some insight, they do not offer the same level of confidence as a technical assessment. Relying on the vendor's assertion of compliance without verification is not advisable.

118. A company has established a third-party risk management program and is evaluating a new vendor. Which of the following risk mitigation strategies would be the MOST effective in managing the risks associated with the vendor?

A. Implementing a formal vendor selection process
B. Requiring the vendor to provide proof of insurance coverage
C. Establishing a service-level agreement with the vendor
D. Conducting regular security audits of the vendor

Answer: C. Establishing a service-level agreement with the vendor
Explanation: Establishing a service-level agreement (SLA) with the vendor is the most effective risk mitigation strategy in this scenario. An SLA clearly defines the vendor's responsibilities, performance metrics, and consequences for non-compliance, providing a legally binding contract that holds the vendor accountable for maintaining security standards. While other options, such as vendor selection processes and security audits, can contribute to risk management, they do not provide the same level of enforceability as an SLA.

119. A security analyst is preparing a compliance report for an organization's management. The analyst is required to include the following information:
- A description of the compliance issue
- The potential impact on the organization
- Recommendations for remediation
- A prioritization of the issue based on severity

Which of the following should the analyst include in the "potential impact on the organization" section?

A. The technical details of the compliance issue
B. The legal and regulatory penalties for non-compliance
C. The steps taken to mitigate the compliance issue
D. The current status of the compliance issue

Answer: B. The legal and regulatory penalties for non-compliance
Explanation: In a compliance report, the potential impact on the organization should include the legal and regulatory penalties for non-compliance, as these are the consequences that the organization may face if it does not adhere to the relevant regulations or standards.

120. A company's internal compliance reporting system should NOT include which of the following?

A. A clear and accessible method for employees to report concerns or violations
B. A system for tracking and resolving reported issues
C. A yearly audit conducted by an external third party
D. A direct line of communication to the CEO for any employee

Correct Answer: C. Explanation: While an external audit can be a valuable tool for assessing a company's compliance, it should not be the only method for evaluating the effectiveness of an internal compliance reporting system. An effective internal compliance reporting system should include clear and accessible methods for employees to report concerns or violations, a system for tracking and resolving reported issues, and a direct line of communication to the CEO for any employee.

121. A company is required to comply with the European Union's General Data Protection Regulation (GDPR) and the Health Insurance Portability and Accountability Act (HIPAA) in the United States. What should the company do to ensure compliance with both regulations?

A. Implement a single set of policies and procedures that meet the requirements of both regulations.
B. Separate the data subject to GDPR and HIPAA and implement different policies and procedures for each.
C. Consult with legal counsel to determine the most stringent requirements and implement those across the organization.
D. Ignore the regulations and hope for the best.

Answer: C. Explanation: Companies must comply with the most stringent requirements of each regulation to ensure adherence to both. Consulting with legal counsel is the best approach to determine these requirements and implement appropriate policies and procedures.

122. A multinational corporation is subject to the Sarbanes-Oxley (SOX) regulation in the United States and the Basel III capital rules in the European Union. What should the corporation do to ensure compliance with both regulations?

A. Implement a single set of policies and procedures that meet the requirements of both regulations.
B. Separate the financial reporting subject to SOX and Basel III and implement different policies and procedures for each.
C. Consult with legal counsel to determine the most stringent requirements and implement those across the organization.
D. Ignore the regulations and hope for the best.

Answer: C. Consult with legal counsel to determine the most stringent requirements and implement those across the organization.
Explanation: As with the previous scenario, companies must comply with the most stringent requirements of each regulation. Consulting with legal counsel is the best approach to determine these requirements and implement appropriate policies and procedures.

123. A healthcare organization is found to be non-compliant with the Health Insurance Portability and Accountability Act (HIPAA) and faces fines. What is the maximum fine that can be imposed on the organization?

A. $10,000
B. $50,000
C. $100,000
D. $1,500,000

Correct Answer: D. Explanation: HIPAA fines for non-compliance can range from $100 to $50,000 per violation, depending on the level of negligence. The maximum penalty for a single violation is $1,500,000.

124. A company that has an annual revenue of 15 billion euros fails to comply with the General Data Protection Regulation (GDPR) and is found to have violated data privacy rights. What is the maximum fine that can be imposed on the company?

   A. 10 million euros
   B. 20 million euros
   C. 40 million euros
   D. 60 million euros

Correct Answer: D. Explanation: GDPR imposes fines of up to 4% of a company's global annual revenue for the preceding financial year **or** €20 million (whichever is higher) for violations of data privacy rights.

125. A company has failed to comply with regulatory requirements and is facing sanctions. Which of the following consequences is the company likely to experience?

   A. Increased revenue
   B. Improved brand reputation
   C. Legal penalties and fines
   D. Enhanced customer loyalty

Correct Answer: C. Explanation: When a company fails to comply with regulatory requirements, it is likely to face legal penalties and fines as a consequence. This is because non-compliance with regulations can lead to legal action, which may result in financial penalties and other sanctions.

126. A company has experienced a data breach, and customer information has been leaked. The company is now facing negative publicity and loss of customer trust. Which of the following best describes the consequence of non-compliance in this scenario?

A. Reputational damage
B. Financial loss
C. Regulatory fines
D. Legal penalties

Correct Answer: A. Explanation: In this scenario, the company has faced negative publicity and loss of customer trust due to the data breach, which is a consequence of non-compliance with data security regulations. Reputational damage is a common consequence of non-compliance, as it can lead to a loss of customer trust, negative publicity, and damage to the company's brand.

127. A company faces a lawsuit for violating data protection regulations. The potential consequence of non-compliance in this scenario is:

A. Loss of license
B. Fines and penalties
C. Reputation damage
D. Increased regulatory scrutiny

Correct Answer: B. Explanation: Fines and penalties are a common consequence of non-compliance with data protection regulations. Companies that fail to adhere to these regulations may face legal action, resulting in financial penalties and other sanctions.

128. A healthcare organization fails to comply with the Health Insurance Portability and Accountability Act (HIPAA) regulations. The potential consequence of non-compliance in this scenario is:

A. Loss of license
B. Fines and penalties
C. Reputation damage
D. Increased regulatory scrutiny

Correct Answer: A. Explanation: In the healthcare industry, non-compliance with HIPAA regulations can lead to severe consequences, including the loss of license to operate. HIPAA violations can result in fines, penalties, and even criminal charges in some cases.

129. A company discovers that it has failed to comply with a contractual obligation to implement a specific security measure. The company is now facing legal action from the client. What is the most likely consequence of this non-compliance?

    A. Loss of client trust
    B. Contract termination
    C. Financial penalties
    D. Loss of intellectual property

Correct Answer: B. Explanation: Contractual non-compliance can lead to various consequences, including contract termination. In this scenario, the company's failure to implement the required security measure has resulted in legal action from the client, which could ultimately lead to the termination of the contract.

130. Which of the following is NOT a component of due diligence in the context of compliance?

    A. Identifying relevant laws, regulations, and policies
    B. Assessing the organization's compliance with these rules
    C. Implementing measures to prevent and detect violations
    D. Ignoring potential compliance issues

Correct Answer: D. ignoring potential compliance issues
Explanation: Due diligence is the effort made by an organization to comply with all relevant laws, regulations, and policies. It involves identifying relevant rules, assessing the organization's compliance, and implementing measures to prevent and detect violations. Ignoring potential compliance issues is not a part of due diligence, as it contradicts the purpose of ensuring adherence to the rules.

131. A security analyst is monitoring the network for compliance with data protection regulations. Identify the due care action that the analyst should take:

A. Implement a new intrusion detection system
B. Review logs for unauthorized access to sensitive data
C. Update the company's security policies
D. Conduct a penetration test of the network

Answer: B. Review logs for unauthorized access to sensitive data
Explanation: Due care in compliance monitoring involves taking reasonable steps to ensure adherence to regulations and policies. Reviewing logs for unauthorized access to sensitive data is a due care action that helps identify potential breaches and ensures that the organization is taking appropriate measures to protect sensitive information.

132. A technology company is developing a new software product and wants to ensure that the product meets the security requirements of its clients. Which of the following attestation methods is the most suitable for the company to use?

A. Management assertion
B. Employee self-assessment
C. Third-party attestation
D. Internal audit

Answer: C. Explanation: Third-party attestation involves an independent party, such as a security consultant, assessing the software product's security features and their effectiveness. This method provides an objective evaluation of the product's security, ensuring that it meets the security requirements of the clients.

133. A compliance officer is reviewing the company's policies and procedures to ensure they align with industry regulations. Which of the following actions should the compliance officer take if they identify a policy that is not in compliance with the regulations?

A. Ignore the non-compliant policy and hope it doesn't cause any issues
B. Update the policy to align with the regulations
C. Consult with legal counsel to determine the best course of action
D. Implement a new policy without considering the regulations

Correct Answer: B. Explanation: When a compliance officer identifies a policy that is not in compliance with industry regulations, they should update the policy to align with the regulations. Ignoring the non-compliant policy and hoping it doesn't cause any issues is not a responsible approach, as it could lead to legal consequences and damage the company's reputation. Consulting with legal counsel may be helpful in some cases, but the primary action should be to update the policy to ensure compliance. Implementing a new policy without considering the regulations could lead to further non-compliance issues.

134. Which of the following is a benefit of automating compliance monitoring?

A. Reducing the need for employee training
B. Improving the accuracy and efficiency of compliance monitoring
C. Decreasing the number of compliance issues
D. Eliminating the need for manual processes

Correct Answer: B. Explanation: Automating compliance monitoring can improve the accuracy and efficiency of the process by reducing the possibility of human error and increasing the speed at which compliance issues can be identified and addressed. Automation also allows organizations to focus their resources on more strategic initiatives, as opposed to manual processes, which can be time-consuming and prone to human error.

135. A security professional is tasked with ensuring that the company's privacy policy is up-to-date and compliant with relevant regulations. Which of the following actions should the security professional take?

A. Review the company's privacy policy and compare it with the applicable regulations
B. Implement a privacy impact assessment (PIA)
C. Train employees on data handling best practices
D. Conduct a penetration test of the company's network

Answer: A. Explanation: Ensuring compliance with relevant regulations is crucial for avoiding legal consequences and maintaining trust with customers. Regularly reviewing and updating the company's privacy policy helps ensure that it remains compliant with the latest regulations and reflects the company's current data handling practices.

136. A company is developing an online service targeting children under 13 years old. Which of the following actions should be taken to comply with Children's Online Privacy Protection Act (COPPA)?

A. Age-gate the website to prevent access by users under 13.
B. Obtain verifiable parental consent before collecting personal information.
C. Implement data minimization techniques to limit the amount of personal information collected.
D. Encrypt all collected personal information to ensure its security.

Answer: B. Explanation: COPPA mandates that websites and online services directed to children under 13 must obtain verifiable parental consent before collecting personal information. While age-gating, data minimization, and encryption are important security measures, they do not replace the need for obtaining parental consent.

137. A website is found to be in violation of Children's Online Privacy Protection Act (COPPA). Which of the following penalties may be imposed?

   A. A fine of up to $10,000 per violation.
   B. A fine of up to $2,000 per violation.
   C. A fine of up to $5,000 per violation.
   D. A fine of up to $1,000 per violation.

Answer: A. Explanation: Violations of COPPA can result in penalties of up to $10,000 per violation. The FTC may bring an enforcement action against the website for non-compliance, leading to financial penalties and other corrective actions.

138. A company that processes credit card payments is required to comply with Payment Card Industry Data Security Standard (PCI DSS). Which of the following security measures should the company implement to ensure compliance?

   A. Implement a firewall and router
   B. Encrypt data transmissions
   C. Regularly update antivirus software
   D. Enforce a strong password policy

Answer: B. Explanation: PCI DSS requires organizations to encrypt cardholder data that is transmitted across open, public networks. Encrypting data transmissions helps protect sensitive information from unauthorized access or disclosure during transmission.

139. A retailer stores customer credit card information in a database. According to Payment Card Industry Data Security Standard (PCI DSS), which of the following practices should the retailer follow?

A. Store the card verification value (CVV) code
B. Mask the primary account number (PAN)
C. Retain expired credit card information
D. Store sensitive authentication data

Answer: B. Mask the primary account number (PAN)
Explanation: Payment Card Industry Data Security Standard (PCI DSS) prohibits the storage of sensitive authentication data, including the CVV code, after authorization. Masking the PAN ensures that only the first six and last four digits of the credit card number are displayed, reducing the risk of unauthorized access to the full card number.

140. A patient is being transferred to a contract nursing home for further care. The nursing home may be provided with individually identifiable healthcare information for the:

A. Patient's medical history
B. Patient's HIV/AIDS status
C. Patient's drug abuse history
D. Patient's alcoholism history

Answer: A. Explanation: Health Insurance Portability and Accountability Act (HIPAA) allows the disclosure of individually identifiable health information to outside healthcare providers, such as nursing homes, for treatment purposes without a written authorization by the patient.

141. A government agency is implementing a new security system to protect sensitive information. Which of the following is the primary objective of Federal Information Security Management Act (FISMA)?

A. Ensuring the confidentiality of sensitive information
B. Ensuring the availability of the new security system
C. Ensuring the integrity of the new security system
D. Ensuring the agency follows proper risk management procedures

Answer: D. Explanation: Federal Information Security Management Act (FISMA) aims to ensure that federal agencies follow proper risk management procedures to protect sensitive information. This includes implementing security controls, assessing security controls, and monitoring the effectiveness of security controls. While confidentiality, availability, and integrity are important aspects of information security, FISMA's primary objective is to ensure that agencies follow appropriate risk management procedures to protect their information systems and information.

142. A company discovers a data breach involving the personal data of its customers. According to General Data Protection Regulation (GDPR), which of the following actions should the company take?

A. Notify the customers affected by the breach
B. Notify the supervising authority
C. Encrypt the affected data
D. Conduct a risk assessment

Answer: B. Explanation: According to General Data Protection Regulation (GDPR), organizations must report data breaches to the relevant supervising authority within 72 hours.

143. A company is developing a new software product that will process the personal data of its customers. According to General Data Protection Regulation (GDPR), which of the following measures should the company implement in the design phase of the product development process?

A. Data minimization
B. Pseudonymization
C. Encryption
D. All of the above

Answer: D. Explanation: General Data Protection Regulation (GDPR), requires organizations to implement appropriate technical and organizational measures to ensure the protection of personal data. Data minimization, pseudonymization, and encryption are some of the measures that can be implemented to achieve this goal.

144. A financial services company is developing a new mobile application for customers to access their accounts and perform transactions. Which of the following security measures should be prioritized during the development process?

A. Implementing multi-factor authentication
B. Ensuring the application is compatible with various mobile devices
C. Implementing a mechanism for users to provide feedback on the application
D. Ensuring the application is visually appealing and user-friendly

Answer: A. Implementing multi-factor authentication
Explanation: Multi-factor authentication is a crucial security measure for protecting financial information, as it adds an additional layer of security beyond just a password. This helps prevent unauthorized access to customer accounts and reduces the risk of fraud. While the other options are important for user experience, they should not take precedence over security measures during the development process.

145. A company has experienced a data breach, and an investigation is underway to determine the type of information that was compromised. Which of the following is NOT considered Personally Identifiable Information (PII)?

A. Social Security numbers
B. Employee work email addresses
C. Company's quarterly financial reports
D. Customer names

Answer: B. Explanation: PII is any information that can be used to identify, contact, or locate an individual, either alone or combined with other information. In this case, employee work email addresses are not considered PII because they are associated with the company and not specific to an individual.

146. A healthcare organization wants to implement a new system to store and manage Protected Health Information (PHI). Which of the following should be their primary concern?

A. Ensuring the system is user-friendly
B. Ensuring the system complies with HIPAA requirements
C. Ensuring the system is cost-effective
D. Ensuring the system is compatible with other software

Answer: B. Ensuring the system complies with HIPAA requirements
Explanation: The primary concern when implementing a new system to store and manage Protected Health Information (PHI) should be ensuring compliance with HIPAA requirements, as HIPAA sets the standard for protecting sensitive patient data. While user-friendliness, cost-effectiveness, and compatibility with other software are important considerations, they should not take precedence over HIPAA compliance.

147. A company is expanding its operations internationally and is concerned about privacy and legal implications. Which of the following is the best approach to address these concerns?

A. Implement a global privacy policy that complies with the strictest privacy laws in all countries where the company operates.
B. Establish separate privacy policies for each country, tailored to the specific legal requirements of each jurisdiction.
C. Rely on the company's existing privacy policy, assuming that it already covers all necessary legal requirements.
D. Ignore privacy laws and focus on implementing the most secure technical solutions.

Correct Answer: A. Explanation: A global privacy policy that complies with the strictest privacy laws in all countries where the company operates is the best approach to address privacy and legal implications. This approach ensures that the company is in compliance with the most stringent privacy regulations, reducing the risk of legal issues and penalties. It also demonstrates a commitment to protecting user privacy, which can enhance the company's reputation and trust with its customers

148. Which of the following best describes the main difference between a controller and a processor in the context of the General Data Protection Regulation (GDPR)?

A. Controllers collect data, while processors store data.
B. Controllers determine the purpose and means of processing personal data, while processors only process personal data on behalf of a controller.
C. Controllers are responsible for data security, while processors are responsible for data privacy.
D. Controllers are the owners of the data, while processors are the custodians of the data.

Correct Answer: B. Explanation: Under GDPR, a controller is responsible for determining the purpose and means of processing personal data, while a processor is responsible for processing personal data on behalf of a controller.

149. A software company has developed a new application that stores user data in the cloud. Who owns the data in this scenario?

A. The software company owns the data.
B. The users own the data.
C. The cloud service provider owns the data.
D. The data is public and has no owner.

Answer: B. Explanation: The users are providing their data to the application, which is then stored in the cloud. The users have a vested interest in the data and its protection, and the software company has a duty to protect the data as it is handling the information on behalf of the users.

150. A research institution has collaborated with a technology company to analyze shared data. Who owns the data in this scenario?

A. The research institution owns the data.
B. The technology company owns the data.
C. Both the research institution and the technology company own the data.
D. The data is public and has no owner.

Answer: C. Explanation: In this scenario, both the research institution and the technology company have a vested interest in the data and its protection. They are working together to analyze the data, and both parties have a duty to protect the data as they are handling the information on behalf of each other.

151. An organization is implementing a data retention policy. Which of the following factors should be considered when determining the retention period for different types of data?

A. The cost of storing the data
B. The legal and regulatory requirements
C. The business value of the data
D. The technical feasibility of data retention

Answer: B. Explanation: When determining the retention period for different types of data, the primary factor to consider is the legal and regulatory requirements. Organizations must comply with various laws and regulations, such as the Health Insurance Portability and Accountability Act (HIPAA) or the Sarbanes-Oxley Act (SOX), which dictate how long certain types of data must be retained.

152. A company is developing a data retention policy. Which of the following best practices should be included in the policy?

A. Encrypting all data stored by the organization
B. Implementing a tiered storage strategy
C. Regularly reviewing and updating the policy
D. Storing all data in a single, centralized location

Answer: C. Explanation: A data retention policy should be regularly reviewed and updated to ensure that it remains compliant with the latest legal and regulatory requirements and aligns with the organization's business needs. This includes staying informed about changes in relevant laws and regulations, as well as periodically assessing the effectiveness of the policy.

153. A company has implemented a data retention policy to comply with regulatory requirements. Which of the following is the primary goal of this policy?

A. To ensure that all data is retained indefinitely
B. To determine the type of data that needs to be retained
C. To establish a schedule for data deletion
D. To minimize the risk of data breaches

Answer: B. Explanation: A data retention policy is designed to determine the type of data that needs to be retained and for how long, based on legal, regulatory, and business requirements. This policy helps organizations comply with relevant laws and regulations, manage risks, and ensure proper data management.

154. Which of the following is NOT a reason for granting the Right to be Forgotten?

A. Protecting personal privacy
B. Preventing identity theft
C. Ensuring accurate and up-to-date information
D. Avoiding embarrassment or inconvenience

Correct Answer: D. Explanation: The Right to be Forgotten is primarily about protecting personal privacy, preventing identity theft, and ensuring accurate and up-to-date information. While it may indirectly help avoid embarrassment or inconvenience, these are not the primary reasons for granting this right.

155. A company's audit committee is reviewing the organization's financial statements and internal controls. They identify a significant deficiency in the company's IT system that could lead to financial misstatements. According to the Sarbanes-Oxley (SOX) Act, what should the audit committee do?

A. Ignore the deficiency since it is an IT issue
B. Inform the full board of directors and management in writing
C. Hire an external IT consultant to fix the issue
D. Implement additional IT training for the accounting department

Correct answer is B. Explanation: According to the Sarbanes-Oxley (SOX) Act, the audit committee is responsible for overseeing the company's financial reporting and internal controls, including those related to IT systems. In this case, the correct answer is (b) Inform the full board of directors and management in writing, as the audit committee is required to report significant deficiencies to the appropriate parties.

156. A company has recently been experiencing a series of cyberattacks, and management is concerned about the security of their network. They have decided to perform an external cyber audit and assessment. Which of the following is the primary goal of this audit and assessment?

A. To evaluate the effectiveness of existing security controls
B. To identify and fix vulnerabilities in the network
C. To determine compliance with relevant industry standards
D. To assess the company's overall security posture

Answer: D. Explanation: The primary goal of an external cyber audit and assessment is to evaluate the effectiveness of existing security controls, identify and fix vulnerabilities in the network, and determine compliance with relevant industry standards. By doing so, the company can assess its overall security posture and identify areas for improvement.

157. A company has recently undergone a regulatory external cyber audit. The auditor has identified several vulnerabilities in the company's network and systems. The auditor has also provided recommendations for mitigating these vulnerabilities. The company is now required to:

A. Implement the recommended mitigations immediately
B. Submit a detailed plan outlining how they will address the identified vulnerabilities
C. Ignore the recommendations and wait for the next audit
D. Implement the recommended mitigations only if they are legally required

Answer: B. Explanation: Companies are typically required to address the findings of a regulatory external cyber audit by submitting a detailed plan outlining how they will address the identified vulnerabilities. This plan is often referred to as a "Plan of Action and Milestones" (POA&M) and is used to track the progress of implementing the necessary security controls and mitigations.

158. A company has recently undergone an external cyber audit. The auditor has identified a critical vulnerability in the company's network. The vulnerability allows attackers to gain unauthorized access to sensitive data by exploiting a misconfigured network device. The auditor recommends implementing a patch to fix the vulnerability. Which of the following actions should the company take to address the auditor's recommendation?

A. Ignore the recommendation, as the company's security team believes the vulnerability is not significant.
B. Apply the patch immediately to mitigate the risk.
C. Schedule a meeting with the auditor to discuss the potential impact of applying the patch.
D. Conduct a risk assessment to determine the likelihood of the vulnerability being exploited.

Answer: B. Explanation: Applying the patch immediately is the correct course of action, as it addresses the identified vulnerability and reduces the risk of unauthorized access to sensitive data. The company should prioritize implementing the auditor's recommendation to ensure the security of its network and data.

159. A penetration tester has identified an open port on a target machine and wants to exploit it. Which of the following steps should the tester take next?

A. Report the vulnerability to the system administrator
B. Attempt to gain access to the system through the open port
C. Perform a risk analysis on the target system
D. Conduct a vulnerability assessment on the target system

Answer: B. Explanation: In a penetration testing scenario, the tester's goal is to identify vulnerabilities and exploit them to gain access to the system. The correct answer is to attempt gaining access to the system through the open port

160. Which of the following is an example of tailgating in a physical penetration test?

A. Exploiting an open wireless network
B. Gaining access to a system through a known vulnerability
C. Following an employee into a restricted area
D. Using a fake ID to gain access to a secure facility

Answer: C. Explanation: Tailgating is a technique used in physical penetration tests where an attacker follows an authorized person into a restricted area to gain unauthorized access.

161. What is the primary goal of a physical penetration test?

A. To identify vulnerabilities in software applications
B. To assess the effectiveness of security controls in a facility
C. To exploit vulnerabilities in a network
D. To gain unauthorized access to sensitive data

Answer: B. Explanation: The primary goal of a physical penetration test is to evaluate the effectiveness of security controls in a facility and identify potential vulnerabilities that could lead to unauthorized access or compromise.

162. Which of the following best describes the difference between offensive and defensive penetration testing?

A. Offensive penetration testing focuses on attacking the network, while defensive penetration testing focuses on securing the network.
B. Offensive penetration testing is performed by attackers, while defensive penetration testing is performed by the network owner.
C. Offensive penetration testing uses open-source tools, while defensive penetration testing uses commercial tools.
D. Offensive penetration testing is performed before a network is deployed, while defensive penetration testing is performed after the network is deployed.

Answer: A. Explanation: Offensive penetration testing, also known as black-box testing, is performed from the perspective of an attacker, attempting to compromise the system and gain unauthorized access. On the other hand, defensive penetration testing, also known as white-box testing, is performed from the perspective of the network owner, focusing on identifying vulnerabilities and implementing security measures to protect the system.

163. Which of the following best describes the main difference between offensive and integrated penetration testing?

A. Offensive penetration testing focuses on exploiting vulnerabilities, while integrated penetration testing focuses on finding and fixing them.
B. Offensive penetration testing is performed by external experts, while integrated penetration testing is performed by internal staff.
C. Offensive penetration testing uses open-source tools, while integrated penetration testing uses commercial tools.
D. Offensive penetration testing is focused on compliance, while integrated penetration testing is focused on security.

Correct Answer: A. Explanation: Offensive penetration testing, also known as black box testing, simulates an attack on a system or network to identify vulnerabilities and exploit them. The goal is to gain unauthorized access to sensitive data, features, or administrative functions. On the other hand, integrated penetration testing combines black box testing with white box testing, which involves having knowledge of the internal workings of the system. This approach aims to find and fix vulnerabilities, rather than just exploiting them.

164. A penetration tester is hired to assess the security of a company's network and is given full knowledge of the network architecture and system details. Which type of penetration testing is the tester performing?

A. Offensive Penetration Testing
B. Integrated Penetration Testing
C. Grey Box Testing
D. White Box Testing

Correct Answer: D. White Box Testing
Explanation: White box testing, also known as clear box testing or glass box testing, is a form of penetration testing where the tester has full knowledge of the system, including its architecture, design, and implementation. This type of testing is typically performed by internal staff or contractors who have access to the system's internals. In the given scenario, the tester is hired to assess the security of a company's network and is given full knowledge of the network architecture and system details, which aligns with the definition of white box testing.

165. A penetration tester is hired to test the security of a company's network. The tester has full knowledge of the network architecture, user names, and some passwords. Which type of penetration testing is this?

A. Unknown environment penetration testing
B. Known environment penetration testing
C. Partially known penetration testing
D. Fully known penetration testing

Answer: C. Partially known penetration testing

Explanation: In this scenario, the tester has some knowledge of the network architecture, user names, and some passwords, but not all the necessary information to completely compromise the system. This makes it a partially known penetration testing.

166. A penetration tester is hired to test the security of a company's network. The tester has no knowledge of the network architecture, user names, or passwords. Which type of penetration testing is this?

A. Unknown environment penetration testing
B. Known environment penetration testing
C. Partially known penetration testing
D. Fully known penetration testing

Answer: A. Unknown environment penetration testing

Explanation: In this scenario, the tester has no knowledge of the network architecture, user names, or passwords, making it an unknown environment penetration testing.

167. A penetration tester is hired to test the security of a company's network. The company provides the tester with no information about their network infrastructure or security measures. Which type of penetration testing is this?

A. Unknown Penetration Testing
B. Known Environment Penetration Testing
C. Black Box Penetration Testing
D. White Box Penetration Testing

Answer: A. Unknown Penetration Testing

Explanation: In unknown penetration testing, the tester has no knowledge of the target network and its security measures. This type of testing simulates the situation where an attacker has no prior knowledge of the target environment, making it a more realistic assessment of the organization's security posture.

168. A penetration tester is hired to test the security of a company's network. The company provides the tester with full access to their network infrastructure and details about their security measures. Which type of penetration testing is this?

A. Unknown Penetration Testing
B. Known Environment Penetration Testing
C. Black Box Penetration Testing
D. White Box Penetration Testing

Answer: B. Known Environment Penetration Testing
Explanation: In known environment penetration testing, the tester has full knowledge of the target network and its security measures. This type of testing is often performed by internal employees or contractors who have access to the organization's security information.

169. An attacker is trying to gather information about a target network using a reconnaissance tool. Which of the following tools is most likely to be used for this purpose?

A. Metasploit
B. Nmap
C. Wireshark
D. Burp Suite

Answer: B. Explanation: Nmap (Network Mapper) is an open-source tool used for network discovery and security auditing. It is commonly used for reconnaissance purposes to gather information about target networks, such as host detection, service identification, and operating system detection.

170. A penetration tester is trying to gain unauthorized access to a system using a compromised set of credentials. Which of the following techniques should the tester use?

A. Brute Force Attack
B. Dictionary Attack
C. Credential Stuffing
D. Social Engineering

Answer: C. Explanation: Credential Stuffing is a technique used to gain unauthorized access to a system by using a set of compromised credentials, such as usernames and passwords, to log in to other systems. This method relies on the reuse of credentials across multiple platforms, making it a popular choice for attackers.

171. Which of the following is a benefit of passive reconnaissance?

A. Gaining more detailed information about the target system or network
B. Lower risk of detection
C. Exploiting vulnerabilities in the target system or network
D. Launching a direct attack on the target system or network

Answer: B. Lower risk of detection
Explanation: Passive reconnaissance involves gathering information from publicly available sources without actively interacting with the target, which results in a lower risk of detection compared to active reconnaissance.

172. Which of the following is an example of Active Reconnaissance in the context of penetration testing?

A. Observing the target network using a network scanner like Nmap
B. Analyzing the target network using a vulnerability scanner like Nessus
C. Performing a social engineering attack to gain access to sensitive information
D. Exploiting a known vulnerability in a network service to gain unauthorized access

Correct Answer: Explanation: Active Reconnaissance involves actively engaging with the target network to gather information about its topology, services, and vulnerabilities. Using a network scanner like Nmap is an example of Active Reconnaissance because it actively probes the target network to identify active hosts, open ports, and running services.

173. What is the primary purpose of Active Reconnaissance in penetration testing?

A. To gain unauthorized access to sensitive data
B. To identify vulnerabilities and potential attack vectors
C. To exploit weaknesses in network security
D. To demonstrate the effectiveness of security controls

Correct Answer: B. Explanation: The primary purpose of Active Reconnaissance is to gather information about the target network and identify potential vulnerabilities and attack vectors. This information can then be used to plan and execute a penetration test, ultimately helping to improve the security posture of the organization.

174. An employee has been found to be accessing sensitive customer data without authorization. Which of the following actions should be taken first?

A. Terminate the employee's access to the system
B. Confront the employee about the unauthorized access
C. Investigate the employee's background and work history
D. Notify the company's legal team of the situation

Correct Answer: A. Explanation: Terminating the employee's access to the system is the first step in mitigating the insider threat. It prevents further unauthorized access and potential damage to sensitive data while the situation is being investigated.

175.A company provides training to its employees on the proper handling of removable media and cables to ensure data security. Which of the following is the MOST important aspect of this training?

A. Teaching employees how to use different types of removable media and cables
B. Explaining the company's policies and procedures for data handling and storage
C. Demonstrating the correct way to connect and disconnect cables and media
D. Encouraging employees to share removable media and cables with their colleagues

Answer: B. Explanation: The most important aspect of training employees on removable media and cables is to ensure they understand the company's policies and procedures for data handling and storage. This includes understanding the proper handling, storage, and disposal of sensitive information, as well as the risks associated with using removable media and cables. While teaching employees how to use different types of removable media and cables (option a) and demonstrating the correct way to connect and disconnect them (option c) are important, they are secondary to understanding the company's policies and procedures.

176.Which of the following is an example of social engineering in the context of user guidance and training?

A. A malicious email that appears to be from a legitimate source, asking the recipient to click on a link and provide sensitive information.
B. A hacker gaining unauthorized access to a network by exploiting a known vulnerability in the network's security system.
C. An attacker using a brute force attack to guess a user's password.
D. A malicious software program that infects a computer and steals sensitive data.

Correct Answer: A. Explanation: Social engineering is the use of deception to manipulate individuals into revealing sensitive information or performing actions that compromise security. In this case, the malicious email is an example of social engineering because it deceives the recipient into believing it is from a legitimate source, with the goal of obtaining sensitive information.

177. A company is implementing a new security awareness program and wants to ensure that employees understand the importance of security in their daily tasks. Which of the following strategies should be included in the program?

A. Regular security audits
B. Quarterly security awareness training
C. Security reminders in the form of posters and emails
D. Mandatory security certifications for all employees

Answer: B. Explanation: Regular security awareness training, such as quarterly sessions, helps keep security top of mind for employees and ensures they remain informed about the latest threats and security best practices. This approach is more effective than annual or one-time training sessions, as it reinforces the importance of security in employees' daily tasks and helps create a culture of security within the organization.

178. A security administrator is developing a training program for employees to prevent social engineering attacks. Which of the following topics should be included in the training program?

A. How to identify phishing emails
B. Proper use of company-issued devices
C. Implementing strong passwords
D. Disposing of sensitive documents

Answer: A. Explanation: Employees should be trained to identify phishing emails, as these attacks are a common social engineering technique used by cybercriminals to trick users into revealing sensitive information or clicking on malicious links. Recognizing and reporting phishing emails is an essential aspect of operational security and helps protect the organization from potential cyber threats.

179. A company is planning to implement a hybrid work model. Which of the following should be their primary concern regarding the security implications of this decision?

A. Ensuring all employees have access to the necessary hardware and software
B. Protecting sensitive data and information from unauthorized access
C. Ensuring all employees have access to reliable internet connections
D. Providing employees with the necessary ergonomic equipment for their home offices

Correct Answer: B. Explanation: The primary concern when implementing a hybrid work model should be protecting sensitive data and information from unauthorized access. This is because remote work can introduce additional security risks, such as unsecured networks, phishing attacks, and data breaches. While other factors, such as access to hardware and software, reliable internet connections, and ergonomic equipment, are important for employee productivity, they do not directly impact the security of the company's sensitive information.

180. Which of the following is the most effective method for mitigating the security risks associated with hybrid and remote work environments?

A. Implementing strict password policies
B. Providing regular security training and guidance
C. Requiring employees to use company-issued devices
D. Implementing a zero-trust security model

Correct Answer: B. Explanation: Regular security training and guidance is the most effective method for mitigating security risks in hybrid and remote work environments. This is because it helps employees understand the unique security challenges associated with remote work and equips them with the knowledge and skills needed to protect sensitive information and maintain a secure work environment. While other options, such as strict password policies, company-issued devices, and zero-trust security models, can also contribute to security, they are not as comprehensive as regular security training and guidance.

183. A company is developing a new mobile application that processes sensitive user data. Which of the following security awareness practices should they implement during the development process?

A. Implement a secure software development methodology
B. Conduct regular security training for developers
C. Use static code analysis tools to identify potential security vulnerabilities
D. Perform manual security code reviews

Answer: A. Explanation: A secure software development methodology helps ensure that security is considered throughout the entire development process, from planning and design to implementation and maintenance. This approach helps identify and mitigate security risks early in the development process, reducing the likelihood of security vulnerabilities in the final product.

184. A software development team is working on a new cloud-based application. Which of the following security awareness practices should they follow to ensure security during the development process?

A. Implement a formal SDLC (System Development Life Cycle) methodology
B. Conduct regular security training for developers
C. Use a threat modeling tool to identify potential security issues
D. Perform manual security code reviews

Answer: A. Explanation: Implementing a formal SDLC methodology helps ensure that security is considered throughout the entire development process, from planning and design to implementation and maintenance. This approach helps identify and mitigate security risks early in the development process, reducing the likelihood of security vulnerabilities in the final product.

181. A company has just implemented a new security policy and is required to provide training to all employees. Which type of training should the company provide?

A. Initial Training
B. Recurring Training
C. On-the-job Training
D. Vendor-provided Training

Answer: A. Explanation: Initial training is provided to employees when they are first introduced to a new system, process, or policy. In this case, the company has just implemented a new security policy, so all employees need to be trained on the new policy, making initial training the correct choice.

182. A company is planning to provide refresher training to its employees to ensure they are up-to-date with the latest security best practices. Which type of training should the company provide?

A. Initial Training
B. Recurring Training
C. On-the-job Training
D. Vendor-provided Training

Answer: B. Explanation: Recurring training is ongoing training provided to employees to ensure they remain current with regulations and industry best practices. In this case, the company is providing refresher training to its employees to keep them updated with the latest security best practices, making recurring training the correct choice.

185. A company is planning to test its employees' understanding of security awareness practices. Which of the following methods should be used to evaluate the effectiveness of the security awareness program?

A. Conducting a phishing simulation
B. Administering a security awareness assessment
C. Reviewing employee attendance records for security training
D. All of the above

Answer: D. Explanation: Evaluating the effectiveness of a security awareness program can be done through various methods, such as conducting a phishing simulation, administering a security awareness assessment, and reviewing employee attendance records for security training. Phishing simulations help gauge employees' ability to recognize and respond to potential phishing threats. Security awareness assessments can measure employees' understanding of security concepts and their ability to apply them in real-world situations. Reviewing employee attendance records ensures that employees are participating in the training and are exposed to the security awareness program.

186. A company wants to raise employee awareness about the dangers of phishing emails. Which of the following activities should be included in the security awareness program?

A. Sending mock phishing emails to employees
B. Providing employees with a list of known phishing websites
C. Offering training on how to identify and report phishing emails
D. Implementing a phishing email reporting system

Answer: C. Explanation: Training employees on how to identify and report phishing emails is an essential aspect of a security awareness program. It helps employees recognize potential threats and take appropriate action, reducing the risk of successful phishing attacks. Implementing a reporting system alone is not enough; employees need to be trained to recognize and report phishing emails effectively.

About the Author

Kie Yavorsky who goes by the name "Yavo" is the creator of Yavoz.tech. He is a cyber security specialist with 14 years of IT experience who served as a Sergeant in the United States Marine Corps from 2009 to 2017, filling cyber security roles including Cyber Chief, Firewall Admin, Network Engineer, Server Admin, Satcom Admin, Radio Admin, Crypto Electronic Key Management System (EKMS) Manager, SharePoint Webmaster, IT Project Manager and Cyber Security Expert. He has been recognized for leading the communication plan of 266th Pope, Pope Francis to the National Capital Region and the 2011 Presidential State of the Union Address, while stationed at Chemical Biological Incident Response force (CBIRF) in Washington DC. Yavo was also recognized during Operation Key Resolve, Cobra Gold, and other operations in the Asia-Pacific region supporting tens of thousands of users while serving in Okinawa Japan. Yavo then became the Cyber Chief of the infantry battalion 3rd Battalion, 4th Marines. The unit holds the nicknames "Thundering Third"and "Darkside". After the Marine Corps Yavo has received multiple innovation and performance awards in his civilian career serving in roles to include Network Operations Lead in Iwakuni Japan, Lead Network Engineer for Defense Information Systems Agency (DISA), Information System Security Officer (ISSO) for the Nuclear Intercontinental Ballistic Missile (ICBM) Minute Man III program In Ogden Utah, Risk Management Framework (RMF) Security Control Assessor (SCA) for AFRICOM, and Information System Security Officer (ISSO) for EUCOM in Stuttgart Germany. His education includes a Master's Degree in Cybersecurity and Information Assurance from Western Governors University and a Bachelor's Degree in Cyber Security with two concentrations, the first concentration in Information Warfare, and the second concentration in Cyber Connections Management from Norwich University. His industry certifications include the Certified Information Systems Security Professional (CISSP), Certified Ethical Hacker (CEH), CompTIA Cybersecurity Analyst (CySA+), CompTIA Security+, Cisco Certified Network Professional Enterprise (CCNP - Enterprise), Cisco Certified Specialist - Enterprise Core, Cisco Certified Specialist - Enterprise Advanced Infrastructure Implementation, Cisco Certified Network Associate (CCNA) and 44 other IT cyber security training certifications. Yavo is continuously innovating and very passionate about cyber security, leading others, and working as a mentor to aspiring IT professionals.

This book covers ONLY the Fifth domain covered by the exam called "Security Program Management".

This book is intended to be a deep dive of practice questions into only the fifth domain called "Security Program Management" and provide people with a resource to prepare them for the exam. The exam itself has a total of 5 domains. This book is part of a set and there is one book for each domain of the exam. This multi-faceted approach allows for a well-rounded understanding of the material, reinforcing key concepts through different learning modalities and providing practical application through practice questions. If you need more to prepare for the exam I recommend going to **https://topcyberpro.com/** and using the resources there.

About the CompTIA Security+ Exam

The CompTIA Security+ SY0-701 certification is a widely recognized validation of an individual's expertise in the cybersecurity domain. It encompasses the latest cybersecurity trends and techniques, with a focus on core technical skills such as risk assessment and management, incident response, forensics, enterprise networks, hybrid/cloud operations, and security controls. This certification exam evaluates candidates' knowledge and skills related to information security and is highly esteemed in the IT industry, serving as a valuable asset for professionals seeking to establish themselves in the cybersecurity field. This link: **https://comptia.org/testing/testing-policies-procedures** provides information on the policies and procedures related to CompTIA certification exams. The page includes several sections that describe different policies and procedures, including the following.

Test Policies: This section includes information on the CompTIA Candidate Code of Ethics Policy, Candidate Testing Policies, CompTIA Voucher Terms & Conditions, Candidate ID Policy, Certification Retake Policy, Exam Delivery Policies, Continuing Education Policies, Exam Development, Sharing Your Exam Results, Unauthorized Training Materials, Candidate Appeals Process, CompTIA Exam Security Hotline, and CompTIA Data Forensics.

CompTIA Candidate Agreement: This section describes the agreement that all certification candidates must agree to before taking a CompTIA exam. It includes information on modifications to exams and certification requirements, compliance with certification exam policies and the code of ethics, and the consequences of violating the agreement.

Exam Delivery Policies: This section provides information on the policies related to the delivery of CompTIA certification exams. It includes information on delivery exclusions, beta testing, and testing center suspensions.

•**Certification Exam Policies:** This section describes the policies related to CompTIA certification exams, including the tester's consent before taking the exam.

•**Candidate Testing Policies**: This section includes information on accommodations during an exam, exam scoring, exam content, international testing policies, candidate retesting, and candidate photographs.

•**CompTIA Certification Retake Policy:** This section provides information on the policy related to retaking a CompTIA certification exam, including waiting periods, beta examinations, and exam price.

DOMAIN	PERCENTAGE OF EXAMINATION
General Security Concepts	12%
Threats, Vulnerabilities, and Mitigations	22%
Security Architecture	18%
Security Operations	28%
Security Program Management and Oversight	20%

Test Details	What You Need to know
Required exam	SY0-701
Number of questions	Maximum of 90
Types of questions	There are mostly multiple-choice questions and a handful of performance-based questions otherwise referred to as lab-questions. You need to correctly answer at least one performance-based question to pass.
Length of test	90 minutes

DoD 8570, DoD 8140, and why it matters.

One of the major reasons having a CompTIA security+ is so important on your resume is because of DoD 8570 and DoD 8140. These government charts of certifications can be thought about as a bingo chart, and different IT jobs require hiring professionals at different levels. The CompTIA Security+ certification appears multiple times on this bingo chart and allows you to qualify for a wide range of IT roles. A more thorough video explanation can be found at

https://www.YouTube.com/watch?v=i0bL0w2mXY4

DoD 8570 is a directive that governs the information assurance functions of Department of Defense systems and those with access to them. It establishes the policies and responsibilities of Department of Defense information assurance, including training, certification, and workforce management. DoD 8570 is a baseline requirement for access to DoD IT systems, and compliance is required

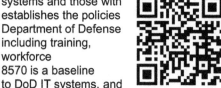

of all authorized users of a DoD Information System, including contractors as well as government employees. DoD 8570 compliance can be achieved by obtaining a number of different certifications, and there is no single certification called '8570.' The certifications required depend on the job category and level of access to DoD information systems. The Defense Information Systems Agency provides a list of DoD-approved baseline certifications. DoD 8570 is not a certification itself, but a policy that outlines cybersecurity certification requirements for specific job categories.

DoD 8570 has been replaced by DoD 8140, but didn't change it much, which expands on 8570 to leverage the Defense Cybersecurity Workforce Framework (DCWF), which draws from the original National Initiative for Cybersecurity Education (NICE) Cybersecurity Workforce Framework (NCWF) and the DoD Joint Cyberspace Training and Certification Standards (JCT&CS).

The 8140 Directive canceled and replaced DoD 8570.01, but it is taking a few years for the Department of Defense to develop a new manual; therefore, the 8570 manual is still current for the time being until it is formally canceled. DoD 8570 was established in 2005 to assess and manage the cybersecurity workforce of the Department of Defense. It was replaced by DoD 8140 in 2015, which expands upon it. DoD 8570 compliance is required of all authorized users of a DoD Information System, including contractors as well as government employees. Compliance can be achieved by obtaining a number of different certifications, and there is no single certification called '8570.' The certifications required depend on the job category and level of access to DoD information systems.

IA Technical		
IAT Level I	**IAT Level II**	**IAT Level III**
A+ CE CCNA-Security CND Network+ CE	CCNA-Security CySA+ CND Security+ CE	CASP CE CCNP CISA CISSP (or Associate)

IA Management		
IAM Level I	**IAM Level II**	**IAM Level III**
CGRC CND Cloud+ Security+ CE	CGRC CASP CISM CISSP (or Associate) CCISO	CISM CISSP (or Associate) CCISO

IA System Architecture and Engineering		
IASAE Level I	**IASAE Level II**	**IASAE Level III**
CASP CE CISSP (or Associate) CSSLP	CASP CE CISSP (or Associate) CSSLP	CISSP-ISSAP CISSP-ISSEP

Cyber Security Service Provider				
CSSP Analyst	**CSSP Infrastructure Support**	**CSSP Incident Responder**	**CSSP Auditor**	**CSSP Manager**
CEH CFR CySA+	CEH CySA+ CND CHFI Cloud+	CEH CFR CHFI Cloud+	CEH CySA+ CISA Cloud+ CHFI	CISM CCISO

Where can you take the exam?

CompTIA Security+ certification exams can be taken either online or in-person at any of the thousands of Pearson VUE test centers located around the world. To find the nearest testing center, visit the CompTIA Certification page on the official Pearson VUE website, select "Find a test center," enter your home address, and click on the search button. Appointments may be made in advance or on the day you wish to test, subject to availability. Pearson VUE offers a variety of scheduling options: online scheduling, scheduling by phone, and scheduling directly through the test center. Before taking a CompTIA exam, all certification candidates will be prompted to agree with the CompTIA Candidate Agreement.

To find a Pearson VUE testing center, you can visit the CompTIA Certification page on the official Pearson VUE website https://home.pearsonvue.com/comptia and then selecting "Find a test center" on the right.

Then, enter your home address and click on the search button. The website will list the nearest testing locations, and you can choose the one that suits you best and proceed with scheduling your exam. Alternatively, you can search for other types of testing centers by using search engines or visiting specific websites. Pearson VUE has a network of more than 5,000 testing centers in 165 countries, and you can find a Pearson VUE Authorized Test Center near you by visiting the Pearson VUE website and using its Test Center Locator. You can also take a photo tour of a Pearson Professional Center on the Pearson VUE website to get an idea of what to expect when you arrive at the testing center. Before taking a CompTIA exam, all certification candidates will be prompted to agree with the CompTIA Candidate Agreement.

Acronyms You'll Encounter

Acronym	Meaning
AAA	Authentication, Authorization, and Accounting
ACL	Access Control List
AES	Advanced Encryption Standard
AES-256	Advanced Encryption Standards 256-bit
AH	Authentication Header
AI	Artificial Intelligence
AIS	Automated Indicator Sharing
ALE	Annualized Loss Expectancy
AP	Access Point
API	Application Programming Interface
APT	Advanced Persistent Threat
ARO	Annualized Rate of Occurrence
ARP	Address Resolution Protocol
ASLR	Address Space Layout Randomization
ATT&CK	Adversarial Tactics, Techniques, and Common Knowledge
AUP	Acceptable Use Policy
AV	Antivirus
BASH	Bourne Again Shell
BCP	Business Continuity Planning
BGP	Border Gateway Protocol
BIA	Business Impact Analysis
BIOS	Basic Input/Output System
BPA	Business Partners Agreement
BPDU	Bridge Protocol Data Unit

BYOD	Bring Your Own Device
CA	Certificate Authority
CAPTCHA	Completely Automated Public Turing Test to Tell Computers and Humans Apart
CAR	Corrective Action Report
CASB	Cloud Access Security Broker
CBC	Cipher Block Chaining
CCMP	Counter Mode/CBC-MAC Protocol
CCTV	Closed-circuit Television
CERT	Computer Emergency Response Team
CFB	Cipher Feedback
CHAP	Challenge Handshake Authentication Protocol
CIA	Confidentiality, Integrity, Availability
CIO	Chief Information Officer
CIRT	Computer Incident Response Team
CMS	Content Management System
COOP	Continuity of Operation Planning
COPE	Corporate Owned, Personally Enabled
CP	Contingency Planning
CRC	Cyclical Redundancy Check
CRL	Certificate Revocation List
CSO	Chief Security Officer
CSP	Cloud Service Provider
CSR	Certificate Signing Request
CSRF	Cross-site Request Forgery
CSU	Channel Service Unit
CTM	Counter Mode
CTO	Chief Technology Officer
CVE	Common Vulnerability Enumeration

CVSS	Common Vulnerability Scoring System
CYOD	Choose Your Own Device
DAC	Discretionary Access Control
DBA	Database Administrator
DDoS	Distributed Denial of Service
DEP	Data Execution Prevention
DES	Digital Encryption Standard
DHCP	Dynamic Host Configuration Protocol
DHE	Diffie-Hellman Ephemeral
DKIM	DomainKeys Identified Mail
DLL	Dynamic Link Library
DLP	Data Loss Prevention
DMARC	Domain Message Authentication Reportingand Conformance
DNAT	Destination Network Address Translation
DNS	Domain Name System
DoS	Denial of Service
DPO	Data Privacy Officer
DRP	Disaster Recovery Plan
DSA	Digital Signature Algorithm
DSL	Digital Subscriber Line
EAP	Extensible Authentication Protocol
ECB	Electronic Code Book
ECC	Elliptic Curve Cryptography
ECDHE	Elliptic Curve Diffie-Hellman Ephemeral
ECDSA	Elliptic Curve Digital Signature Algorithm
EDR	Endpoint Detection and Response

EFS	Encrypted File System
ERP	Enterprise Resource Planning
ESN	Electronic Serial Number
ESP	Encapsulated Security Payload
FACL	File System Access Control List
FDE	Full Disk Encryption
FIM	File Integrity Management
FPGA	Field Programmable Gate Array
FRR	False Rejection Rate
FTP	File Transfer Protocol
FTPS	Secured File Transfer Protocol
GCM	Galois Counter Mode
GDPR	General Data Protection Regulation
GPG	Gnu Privacy Guard
GPO	Group Policy Object
GPS	Global Positioning System
GPU	Graphics Processing Unit
GRE	Generic Routing Encapsulation
HA	High Availability
HDD	Hard Disk Drive
HIDS	Host-based Intrusion Detection System
HIPS	Host-based Intrusion Prevention System
HMAC	Hashed Message Authentication Code
HOTP	HMAC-based One-time Password
HSM	Hardware Security Module
HTML	Hypertext Markup Language
HTTP	Hypertext Transfer Protocol
HTTPS	Hypertext Transfer Protocol Secure
HVAC	Heating, Ventilation Air Conditioning

IaaS	Infrastructure as a Service
IaC	Infrastructure as Code
IAM	Identity and Access Management
ICMP	Internet Control Message Protocol
ICS	Industrial Control Systems
IDEA	International Data Encryption Algorithm
IDF	Intermediate Distribution Frame
IdP	Identity Provider
IDS	Intrusion Detection System
IEEE	Institute of Electrical and Electronics Engineers
IKE	Internet Key Exchange
IM	Instant Messaging
IMAP	Internet Message Access Protocol
IoC	Indicators of Compromise
IoT	Internet of Things
IP	Internet Protocol
IPS	Intrusion Prevention System
IPSec	Internet Protocol Security
IR	Incident Response
IRC	Internet Relay Chat
IRP	Incident Response Plan
ISO	International Standards Organization
ISP	Internet Service Provider
ISSO	Information Systems Security Officer
IV	Initialization Vector
KDC	Key Distribution Center

KEK	Key Encryption Key
L2TP	Layer 2 Tunneling Protocol
LAN	Local Area Network
LDAP	Lightweight Directory Access Protocol
LEAP	Lightweight Extensible Authentication Protocol
MaaS	Monitoring as a Service
MAC	Mandatory Access Control
MAC	Media Access Control
MAC	Message Authentication Code
MAN	Metropolitan Area Network
MBR	Master Boot Record
MD5	Message Digest 5
MDF	Main Distribution Frame
MDM	Mobile Device Management
MFA	Multifactor Authentication
MFD	Multifunction Device
MFP	Multifunction Printer
ML	Machine Learning
MMS	Multimedia Message Service
MOA	Memorandum of Agreement
MOU	Memorandum of Understanding
MPLS	Multi-protocol Label Switching
MSA	Master Service Agreement
MSCHAP	Microsoft Challenge Handshake Authentication Protocol
MSP	Managed Service Provider
MSSP	Managed Security Service Provider
MTBF	Mean Time Between Failures
MTTF	Mean Time to Failure

MTTR	Mean Time to Recover
MTU	Maximum Transmission Unit
NAC	Network Access Control
NAT	Network Address Translation
NDA	Non-disclosure Agreement
NFC	Near Field Communication
NGFW	Next-generation Firewall
NIDS	Network-based Intrusion Detection System
NIPS	Network-based Intrusion Prevention System
NIST	National Institute of Standards & Technology
NTFS	New Technology File System
NTLM	New Technology LAN Manager
NTP	Network Time Protocol
OAUTH	Open Authorization
OCSP	Online Certificate Status Protocol
OID	Object Identifier
OS	Operating System
OSINT	Open-source Intelligence
OSPF	Open Shortest Path First
OT	Operational Technology
OTA	Over the Air
OVAL	Open Vulnerability Assessment Language
P12	PKCS #12
P2P	Peer to Peer
PaaS	Platform as a Service
PAC	Proxy Auto Configuration

PAM	Privileged Access Management
PAM	Pluggable Authentication Modules
PAP	Password Authentication Protocol
PAT	Port Address Translation
PBKDF2	Password-based Key Derivation Function 2
PBX	Private Branch Exchange
PCAP	Packet Capture
PCI DSS	Payment Card Industry Data Security Standard
PDU	Power Distribution Unit
PEAP	Protected Extensible Authentication Protocol
PED	Personal Electronic Device
PEM	Privacy Enhanced Mail
PFS	Perfect Forward Secrecy
PGP	Pretty Good Privacy
PHI	Personal Health Information
PII	Personally Identifiable Information
PIV	Personal Identity Verification
PKCS	Public Key Cryptography Standards
PKI	Public Key Infrastructure
POP	Post Office Protocol
POTS	Plain Old Telephone Service
PPP	Point-to-Point Protocol
PPTP	Point-to-Point Tunneling Protocol
PSK	Pre-shared Key
PTZ	Pan-tilt-zoom
PUP	Potentially Unwanted Program
RA	Recovery Agent
RA	Registration Authority
RACE	Research and Development in Advanced

	Communications Technologies in Europe
RAD	Rapid Application Development
RADIUS	Remote Authentication Dial-in User Service
RAID	Redundant Array of Inexpensive Disks
RAS	Remote Access Server
RAT	Remote Access Trojan
RBAC	Role-based Access Control
RBAC	Rule-based Access Control
RC4	Rivest Cipher version 4
RDP	Remote Desktop Protocol
RFID	Radio Frequency Identifier
RIPEMD	RACE Integrity Primitives Evaluation Message Digest
ROI	Return on Investment
RPO	Recovery Point Objective
RSA	Rivest, Shamir, & Adleman
RTBH	Remotely Triggered Black Hole
RTO	Recovery Time Objective
RTOS	Real-time Operating System
RTP	Real-time Transport Protocol
S/MIME	Secure/Multipurpose Internet Mail Extensions
SaaS	Software as a Service
SAE	Simultaneous Authentication of Equals
SAML	Security Assertions Markup Language
SAN	Storage Area Network
SAN	Subject Alternative Name
SASE	Secure Access Service Edge

SCADA	Supervisory Control and Data Acquisition
SCAP	Security Content Automation Protocol
SCEP	Simple Certificate Enrollment Protocol
SDK	Software Development Kit
SDLC	Software Development Lifecycle
SDLM	Software Development Lifecycle Methodology
SDN	Software-defined Networking
SD-WAN	Software-defined Wide Area Network
SE Linux	Security-enhanced Linux
SED	Self-encrypting Drives
SEH	Structured Exception Handler
SFTP	Secured File Transfer Protocol
SHA	Secure Hashing Algorithm
SHTTP	Secure Hypertext Transfer Protocol
SIEM	Security Information and Event Management
SIM	Subscriber Identity Module
SLA	Service-level Agreement
SLE	Single Loss Expectancy
SMS	Short Message Service
SMTP	Simple Mail Transfer Protocol
SMTPS	Simple Mail Transfer Protocol Secure
SNMP	Simple Network Management Protocol
SOAP	Simple Object Access Protocol
SOAR	Security Orchestration, Automation, Response
SoC	System on Chip
SOC	Security Operations Center
SOW	Statement of Work
SPF	Sender Policy Framework
SPIM	Spam over Internet Messaging

SQL	Structured Query Language
SQLi	SQL Injection
SRTP	Secure Real-Time Protocol
SSD	Solid State Drive
SSH	Secure Shell
SSL	Secure Sockets Layer
SSO	Single Sign-on
STIX	Structured Threat Information eXchange
SWG	Secure Web Gateway
TACACS+	Terminal Access Controller Access Control System
TAXII	Trusted Automated eXchange of Indicator Information
TCP/IP	Transmission Control Protocol/Internet Protocol
TGT	Ticket Granting Ticket
TKIP	Temporal Key Integrity Protocol
TLS	Transport Layer Security
TOC	Time-of-check
TOTP	Time-based One-time Password
TOU	Time-of-use
TPM	Trusted Platform Module
TSIG	Transaction Signature
TTP	Tactics, Techniques, and Procedures
UAT	User Acceptance Testing
UAV	Unmanned Aerial Vehicle
UDP	User Datagram Protocol
UEFI	Unified Extensible Firmware Interface

UEM	Unified Endpoint Management
UPS	Uninterruptable Power Supply
URI	Uniform Resource Identifier
URL	Universal Resource Locator
USB	Universal Serial Bus
USB OTG	USB On the Go
UTM	Unified Threat Management
UTP	Unshielded Twisted Pair
VBA	Visual Basic
VDE	Virtual Desktop Environment
VDI	Virtual Desktop Infrastructure
VLAN	Virtual Local Area Network
VLSM	Variable Length Subnet Masking
VM	Virtual Machine
VoIP	Voice over IP
VPC	Virtual Private Cloud
VPN	Virtual Private Network
VTC	Video Teleconferencing
WAF	Web Application Firewall
WAP	Wireless Access Point
WEP	Wired Equivalent Privacy
WIDS	Wireless Intrusion Detection System
WIPS	Wireless Intrusion Prevention System
WO	Work Order
WPA	Wi-Fi Protected Access
WPS	Wi-Fi Protected Setup
WTLS	Wireless TLS
XDR	Extended Detection and Response
XML	Extensible Markup Language

XOR	Exclusive Or
XSRF	Cross-site Request Forgery
XSS	Cross-site Scripting

Ports and Protocols You'll Encounter
Well-known/System Ports: 0 – 1023

Well-known/System Ports are a range of port numbers from 0 to 1023 that are reserved for specific applications or services. These ports are also known as system ports because they are used by system processes that provide widely used types of network services. Examples of well-known ports include port 21 for FTP, port 22 for SSH, port 23 for Telnet, port 25 for SMTP, port 53 for DNS, port 80 for HTTP, and port 443 for HTTPS. These ports are assigned by the Internet Assigned Numbers Authority (IANA) and are used by transport protocols (TCP, UDP, DCCP, SCTP) to identify an application or service. Well-known ports are different from registered ports (1024-49151) and dynamic or private ports (49152-65535), which are used for user applications and temporary or private ports, respectively. On Unix-like operating systems, a process must execute with superuser privileges to be able to bind a network socket to an IP address using one of the well-known ports.

Port number	Service name	Transport protocol	Description
7	Echo	TCP, UDP	Echo service
19	CHARGEN	TCP, UDP	Character Generator Protocol, has severe vulnerabilities and thus is rarely used nowadays
20	FTP-data	TCP, SCTP	File Transfer Protocol data transfer
21	FTP	TCP, UDP, SCTP	File Transfer Protocol command control
22	SSH/SCP/SFTP	TCP, UDP, SCTP	Secure Shell, secure logins, file transfers (scp, sftp), and port forwarding
23	Telnet	TCP	Telnet protocol, for unencrypted text communications

25	SMTP	TCP	Simple Mail Transfer Protocol, used for email routing between mail servers
42	WINS Replication	TCP, UDP	Microsoft Windows Internet Name Service, vulnerable to attacks on a local network
43	WHOIS	TCP, UDP	Whois service, provides domain-level information
49	TACACS	UDP; can also use TCP but not necessarily on port 49	Terminal Access Controller Access-Control System, provides remote authentication and related services for network access
53	DNS	TCP, UDP	Domain Name System name resolver
67	DHCP/BOOTP	UDP	Dynamic Host Configuration Protocol and its predecessor Bootstrap Protocol Server; server port
68	DHCP/BOOTP	UDP	Dynamic Host Configuration Protocol and its predecessor Bootstrap Protocol Server; client port
69	TFTP	UDP	Trivial File Transfer Protocol

70	Gopher	TCP	Gopher is a communication protocol for distributing, searching, and retrieving documents in Internet Protocol (IP) networks
79	Finger	TCP	Name/Finger protocol and Finger user information protocol, for retrieving and manipulating user information
80	HTTP	TCP, UDP, SCTP	Hypertext Transfer Protocol (HTTP) uses TCP in versions 1.x and 2. HTTP/3 uses QUIC, a transport protocol on top of UDP
88	Kerberos	TCP, UDP	Network authentication system
102	Microsoft Exchange ISO-TSAP	TCP	Microsoft Exchange ISO Transport Service Access Point (TSAP) Class 0 protocol
110	POP3	TCP	Post Office Protocol, version 3 (POP3)
113	Ident	TCP	Identification Protocol, for identifying the user of a particular TCP connection
119	NNTP (Usenet)	TCP	Network News Transfer Protocol
123	NTP	UDP	Network Time Protocol

135	Microsoft RPC EPMAP	TCP, UDP	Microsoft Remote Procedure Call (RPC) Endpoint Mapper (EPMAP) service, for remote system access and management
137	NetBIOS-ns	TCP, UDP	NetBIOS Name Service, used for name registration and resolution
138	NetBIOS-dgm	TCP, UDP	NetBIOS Datagram Service, used for providing access to shared resources
139	NetBIOS-ssn	TCP, UDP	NetBIOS Session Service
143	IMAP	TCP, UDP	Internet Message Access Protocol (IMAP), management of electronic mail messages on a server
161	SNMP-agents (unencrypted)	UDP	Simple network management protocol; agents communicate on this port
162	SNMP-trap (unencrypted)	UDP	Simple network management protocol; listens for asynchronous traps
177	XDMCP	UDP	X Display Manager Control Protocol
179	BGP	TCP	Border Gateway Protocol
194	IRC	UDP	Internet Relay Chat

201	AppleTalk	TCP, UDP	AppleTalk Routing Maintenance. Trojan horses and computer viruses have used UDP port 201.
264	BGMP	TCP, UDP	Border Gateway Multicast Protocol
318	TSP	TCP, UDP	Time Stamp Protocol
381	HP Openview	TCP, UDP	HP performance data collector
383	HP Openview	TCP, UDP	HP data alarm manager
389	LDAP	TCP, UDP	Lightweight directory access protocol
411	(Multiple uses)	TCP, UDP	Direct Connect Hub, Remote MT Protocol
412	(Multiple uses)	TCP, UDP	Direct Connect Client-to-Client, Trap Convention Port
427	SLP	TCP	Service Location Protocol
443	HTTPS (HTTP over SSL)	TCP, UDP, SCTP	Hypertext Transfer Protocol Secure (HTTPS) uses TCP in versions 1.x and 2. HTTP/3 uses QUIC, a transport protocol on top of UDP.
445	Microsoft DS SMB	TCP, UDP	Microsoft Directory Services: TCP for Active Directory, Windows shares; UDP for Server Message Block (SMB) file-sharing

464	Kerberos	TCP, UDP	For password settings on Kerberos
465	SMTP over TLS/SSL, SSM	TCP	Authenticated SMTP over TLS/SSL (SMTPS), URL Rendezvous Directory for Cisco's Source Specific Multicast protocol (SSM)
497	Dantz Retrospect	TCP, UDP	A software suite for backing up operating systems
500	IPSec / ISAKMP / IKE	UDP	Internet Protocol Security / Internet Security Association and Key Management Protocol / Internet Key Exchange
512	rexec	TCP	Remote Process Execution
513	rlogin	TCP	The Unix program rlogin allows users to log in on another host using a network.
514	syslog	UDP	Syslog Protocol, for collecting and organizing all of the log files sent from the various devices on a network
515	LPD/LPR	TCP	Line Printer Daemon protocol, or Line Printer Remote protocol

520	RIP	UDP	Routing Information Protocol, used to find the optimal path between source and destination networks
521	RIPng (IPv6)	UDP	Routing Information Protocol next generation, the IPv6 compatible version of RIP
540	UUCP	TCP	Unix-to-Unix Copy Protocol
548	AFP	TCP	Apple Filing Protocol
554	RTSP	TCP, UDP	Real Time Streaming Protocol
546	DHCPv6	TCP, UDP	Dynamic Host Configuration Protocol version 6. DHCPv6 Clients listen for DHCPv6 messages on UDP port 546.
547	DHCPv6	TCP, UDP	DHCPv6 Servers and DHCPv6 Relay Agents listen for DHCPv6 messages on UDP port 547.
560	rmonitor	UDP	Remote Monitor
563	NNTP over TLS/SSL	TCP, UDP	Network News Transfer Protocol with encryption and verification
587	SMTP	TCP	For email message submission via SMTP
591	FileMaker	TCP	FileMaker Web Companion, the web publishing technology available in FileMaker versions 4-6

593	Microsoft DCOM	TCP, UDP	Distributed Component Object Model (DCOM)
596	SMSD	TCP, UDP	SysMan Station daemon
631	IPP	TCP	Internet Printing Protocol
636	LDAP over TLS/SSL	TCP, UDP	Lightweight Directory Access Protocol over TLS/SSL
639	MSDP (PIM)	TCP	Multicast Source Discovery Protocol, which is part of the Protocol Independent Multicast (PIM) family
646	LDP (MPLS)	TCP, UDP	Label Distribution Protocol, applies to routers capable of Multiprotocol Label Switching (MPLS)
691	Microsoft Exchange	TCP	Microsoft Exchange Routing
860	iSCSI	TCP	Internet Small Computer Systems Interface
873	rsync	TCP	The rsync file synchronization protocol efficiently transfers and synchronizes files between devices and networked computers.
902	VMware Server	TCP, UDP	VMware ESXi, a hypervisor

989	FTPS	TCP	File Transfer Protocol (data) over TLS/SSL
990	FTPS	TCP	File Transfer Protocol (control) over TLS/SSL
993	IMAP over SSL (IMAPS)	TCP	Internet Message Access Protocol over TLS/SSL
995	POP3 over SSL (POP3S)	TCP, UDP	Post Office Protocol 3 over TLS/SSL

Registered Ports are a range of port numbers from 1024 to 49151 that are assigned by the Internet Assigned Numbers Authority (IANA) to specific applications or services. These ports are used by transport protocols (TCP, UDP, DCCP, SCTP) to identify an application or service. Registered ports are also known as user ports because they are assigned to user applications. They are used by applications that are mostly vendor-specific, such as Skype and BitTorrent. Well-known ports (0-1023) are reserved for specific applications or services, while dynamic or private ports (49152-65535) are used for temporary or private ports. The range of registered ports is managed by the IANA, and the registration procedure is defined in document RFC4340, section 19.9. The assignment of a port number does not imply an endorsement of an application or product, and the fact that network traffic is flowing to or from a registered port does not mean that it is "good" traffic. Firewall and system administrators should choose how to configure their systems based on their knowledge of the traffic in question, not whether there is a port number registered or not.

1025	Microsoft RPC	TCP	Microsoft Remote Procedure Call
1026-1029	Windows Messenger	UDP	Windows Messenger popup spam
1080	SOCKS proxy	TCP (or UDP since SOCKS5)	SOCKS stands for Socket Secure. This protocol exchanges network packets between a client and server through a proxy server.
1080	MyDoom	TCP	Computer virus
1194	OpenVPN	TCP, UDP	OpenVPN
1214	KAZAA	TCP	A peer-to-peer file-sharing protocol
1241	Nessus	TCP, UDP	Nessus Security

			Scanner
1311	Dell OpenManage	TCP	Dell EMC OpenManage Server Administrator Web GUI
1337	WASTE	TCP	WASTE peer-to-peer encrypted file-sharing Program
1589	Cisco VQP	TCP, UDP	Cisco VLAN Query Protocol (VQP)
1701	L2TP VPN	TCP	Layer Two Tunneling Protocol Virtual Private Networking
1720	H.323	TCP	H.323 Call Control Signaling, a VoIP call control protocol
1723	Microsoft PPTP	TCP, UDP	Point-to-Point Tunneling Protocol Virtual Private Networking
1725	Steam	UDP	Valve Steam Client uses port 1725
1741	CiscoWorks SNMS 2000	TCP	CiscoWorks Small Network Management Solution web server
1755	MMS	TCP, UDP	Microsoft Media Server
1812	RADIUS	UDP	RADIUS server authentication and authorization
1813	RADIUS	UDP	RADIUS server accounting
1863	(Multiple uses)	TCP, UDP	MSN Messenger, Xbox Live 360
1900	UPnP	UDP	Universal Plug and Play
1985	Cisco HSRP	UDP	Hot Standby Router Protocol
2000	Cisco	TCP	Skinny Client

	SCCP		Control Protocol
2002	Cisco ACS	TCP	Access Control Server
2049	NFS	UDP	Network File Sharing
2082	cPanel	TCP, UDP	cPanel default
2083	radsec, cPanel	TCP, UDP	Secure RADIUS Service (radsec), cPanel default SSL
2100	amiganetfs	TCP	Amiga Network Filesystem
2222	DirectAdmin	TCP	Graphical web hosting control panel
2302	Gaming	UDP	The game HALO uses this port extensively
2483	Oracle	TCP, UDP	Oracle database listening for insecure client connections to the listener, replaces port 1521
2484	Oracle	TCP, UDP	Oracle database listening for SSL client connections to the listener
2745	Bagle.C – Bagle.H	TCP	Computer worms
2967	Symantec AV	TCP, UDP	Symantec System Center agent (SSC-AGENT)
3050	Interbase DB	TCP, UDP	Borland Interbase database
3074	XBOX Live	TCP, UDP	Gaming: Xbox LIVE and Games for Windows – Live
3127	MyDoom	TCP	Computer worm

3128	HTTP Proxy	TCP	Common web proxy server ports: 80, 8080, 3128, 6588
3222	GLBP	TCP, UDP	Gateway Load Balancing Protocol
3260	iSCSI Target	TCP, UDP	Microsoft iSCSI Target Server
3306	MySQL	TCP	MySQL database system
3389	RDP	TCP	Windows Remote Desktop Protocol (Microsoft Terminal Server)
3689	DAAP	TCP	Digital Audio Access Protocol, used by Apple's iTunes and AirPort Express
3690	SVN	TCP, UDP	Apache Subversion, a version control system
3724	World of Warcraft	TCP, UDP	Some Blizzard games, Unofficial Club Penguin Disney online game for kids
3784-3785	Ventrilo VoIP	TCP, UDP	Ventrilo's Voice over Internet Protocol program
4333	mSQL	TCP	Mini SQL server
4444	Blaster	TCP, UDP	Computer worm
4500	IPSec NAT Traversal	UDP	Internet Protocol Security Network Address Translation (NAT) Traversal
4664	Google Desktop	TCP	Google Desktop's built-in HTTP server and indexing software
4672	eMule	UDP	Peer-to-peer file-sharing software

4899	Radmin	TCP	Remote computer control software
5000	UPnP	TCP	Universal Plug and Play
5001	iperf	TCP	Tool for measuring TCP and UDP bandwidth performance
5004-5005	RTP, RTSP	UDP	Real-time Transport Protocol, Real Time Streaming Protocol
5050	Yahoo! Messenger	TCP	Instant messaging service from Yahoo
5060	SIP	TCP, UDP	Session Initiation Protocol
5061	SIP-TLS	TCP	Session Initiation Protocol over TLS
5190	(Multiple uses)	TCP, UDP	ICQ, AIM (AOL Instant Messenger), Apple iChat
5222-5223	XMPP	TCP, UDP	Extensible Messaging and Presence Protocol Client Connection; also used in Google Talk, Jabber, Apple iChat, WhatsApp, etc.
5353	MDNS	UDP	Multicast DNS
5432	PostgreSQL	TCP	PostgreSQL database system
5554	Sasser	TCP	Computer worm
5631-5632	pcAnywhere	UDP	Symantec pcAnywhere
5800	VNC over HTTP	TCP	Virtual Network Computing (VNC)

5900-5999	RFB/VNC Server	TCP, UDP	VNC Remote Frame Buffer RFB protocol
6000	X11	TCP	X Window System protocol for delivering payloads between X clients and servers
6001	X11	UDP	X Window System protocol for delivering payloads between X clients and servers
6112	Diablo	TCP, UDP	Gaming
6129	DameWare	TCP	Remote access software developed by SolarWinds
6257	WinMX	UDP	Windows Music Exchange, peer-to-peer file-sharing freeware
6346-6347	Gnutella2	TCP, UDP	Peer-to-peer network protocol
6379	Redis	TCP	Popular non-relational database management system (NoSql)
6500	GameSpy	TCP, UDP	Gaming
6566	SANE	TCP, UDP	Scanner Access Now Easy
6588	AnalogX	TCP	AnalogX proxy server
6588	HTTP Proxy	TCP	Common web proxy server ports: 80, 8080, 3128, 6588
6665-6669	IRC	TCP	Internet Relay Chat
6679, 6697	IRC over SSL	TCP	Internet Relay Chat
6699	Napster	TCP	Peer-to-peer file-sharing application

6881-6999	BitTorrent	TCP, UDP	BitTorrent uses this range of ports the most often
6891-6901	Windows Live Messenger	TCP, UDP	Alternatively: MSN Messenger
6970	Quicktime	TCP, UDP	QuickTime streaming server
7000	Cassandra	TCP	Inter-node communication within the cluster on Apache Cassandra
7001	Cassandra	TCP	SSL-enabled inter-node communication within the cluster on Apache Cassandra
7199	Cassandra JMX	TCP	Java Management Extensions on Apache Cassandra
7648-7649	CU-SeeMe	TCP, UDP	Internet video conferencing client made by Cornell University
8000	Internet Radio	TCP	Commonly choice of alternate HTTP port for web applications
8080	HTTP Proxy	TCP	Common web proxy server ports: 80, 8080, 3128, 6588
8086	Kaspersky AV	TCP	Kaspersky AV Control Center
8087	Kaspersky AV	UDP	Kaspersky AV Control Center
8118	Privoxy	TCP	Advertisement-filtering Web proxy
8200	VMware Server	TCP, UDP	VMware vSphere Fault Tolerance

8222	VMware Server	TCP, UDP	VMware Server Management User Interface (insecure Web interface).
8500	(Multiple uses)	TCP, UDP	Adobe ColdFusion, Flight Message Transfer Protocol
8767	Teamspeak	UDP	VoIP communication system for online gaming
8866	Bagle.B	TCP	Computer worm
9042	Cassandra	TCP	Apache Cassandra, a NoSql database
9100	PDL	TCP	PDL Data Stream, used for printing to certain network printers
9101-9103	Bacula	TCP, UDP	For automating backup tasks
9119	MXit	TCP, UDP	MXit Instant Messaging (deprecated)
9800	WebDAV	TCP, UDP	Web-based Distributed Authoring and Versioning, an extension of HTTP
9898	Dabber	TCP	Computer worm (Sasser)
9999	Urchin	TCP, UDP	Urchin Web Analytics
10000	(Multiple uses)	TCP, UDP	Network Data Management Protocol; applications: Webmin, BackupExec, Viatalk; gaming: The Matrix Online, Dungeon Fighter

Port	Name	Protocol	Description
10161	SNMP-agents (encrypted)	TCP	Simple network management protocol; agents communicate on this port
10162	SNMP-trap (encrypted)	TCP	Simple network management protocol; listens for asynchronous traps
10113	NetIQ	TCP, UDP	NetIQ Endpoint
10114	NetIQ	TCP, UDP	NetIQ Qcheck
10115	NetIQ	TCP, UDP	NetIQ Endpoint
10116	NetIQ	TCP, UDP	NetIQ VoIP Assessor
11371	OpenPGP	TCP, UDP	OpenPGP HTTP Keyserver
12345	NetBus	TCP	NetBus remote administration tool (Trojan horse)
13720-13721	NetBackup	TCP, UDP	NetBackup request daemon
14567	Battlefield	UDP	Gaming
15118	Dipnet/Odd bob	TCP	Trojan horse
19226	AdminSecure	TCP	Panda Software AdminSecure Communication Agent
19638	Ensim	TCP	Ensim Control Panel
20000	Usermin	TCP, UDP	Web email interface for regular non-root users
24800	Synergy	TCP, UDP	Keyboard/mouse sharing software
25999	Xfire	TCP	Communication tool for gamers (deprecated)

27015	Half-Life	UDP	Gaming
27017	MongoDB	TCP	NoSql database
27374	Sub7	TCP, UDP	Trojan horse
28960	Call of Duty	TCP, UDP	Gaming
31337	Back Orifice	TCP, UDP	Remote administration tool used for Trojan horses
33434+	traceroute	UDP	Utility for displaying paths and measuring transit delays of packets across a network

Dynamic/Private Ports: 49152 – 65535

Dynamic/Private Ports are a range of port numbers from 49152 to 65535 that are not assigned, controlled, or registered. They are used for temporary or private ports and are also known as private or ephemeral ports. These ports are used by clients and not servers. When a client initiates a connection with a server, it chooses a random port number from this range as the source port. This port number is used to direct traffic back to the client. Dynamic ports are assigned to a process or service at the time the port is needed, usually when the process or service is started. Once the process or service is stopped, the port becomes available again for other processes or services to use. Dynamic ports are different from well-known ports (0-1023) and registered ports (1024-49151), which are reserved for specific applications or services.

Summary List of Ports most likely to appear **on any Cyber** Certification **Exam**

Author's Note: *When preparing for a cybersecurity certification exam, it is important to understand commonly used ports and protocols, but it is not necessary to memorize them all. Instead, focus on reviewing and understanding them, and remember that in real-world production environments, you can look up port numbers. It is more likely that you will be given a scenario that describes another aspect of cybersecurity using a port or protocol, and you'll be expected to understand what port or protocol is in the question so that you can answer the underlying scenario question about another security topic. Therefore, it is recommended to focus on ports and protocols as only 10% of your study time while preparing for the exam.*

7	Echo	TCP, UDP	Echo service
20	FTP-data	TCP, SCTP	File Transfer Protocol data transfer
21	FTP	TCP, UDP, SCTP	File Transfer Protocol command control

22	SSH/SCP/SFTP	TCP, UDP, SCTP	Secure Shell, secure logins, file transfers (scp, sftp), and port forwarding
23	Telnet	TCP	Telnet protocol, for unencrypted text communications
25	SMTP	TCP	Simple Mail Transfer Protocol, used for email routing between mail servers
53	DNS	TCP, UDP	Domain Name System name resolver
67	DHCP/BOOTP	UDP	Dynamic Host Configuration Protocol and its predecessor Bootstrap Protocol Server; server port
68	DHCP/BOOTP	UDP	Dynamic Host Configuration Protocol and its predecessor Bootstrap Protocol Server; client port
69	TFTP	UDP	Trivial File Transfer Protocol
80	HTTP	TCP, UDP, SCTP	Hypertext Transfer Protocol (HTTP) uses TCP in versions 1.x and 2. HTTP/3 uses QUIC, a transport protocol on top of UDP
88	Kerberos	TCP, UDP	Network authentication system
110	POP3	TCP	Post Office Protocol, version 3 (POP3)

123	NTP	UDP	Network Time Protocol
137	NetBIOS-ns	TCP, UDP	NetBIOS Name Service, used for name registration and resolution
143	IMAP	TCP, UDP	Internet Message Access Protocol (IMAP), management of electronic mail messages on a server
161	SNMP-agents (unencrypte d)	UDP	Simple network management protocol; agents communicate on this port
194	IRC	UDP	Internet Relay Chat
389	LDAP	TCP, UDP	Lightweight directory access protocol
443	HTTPS (HTTP over SSL)	TCP, UDP, SCTP	Hypertext Transfer Protocol Secure (HTTPS) uses TCP in versions 1.x and 2. HTTP/3 uses QUIC, a transport protocol on top of UDP.
445	Microsoft DS SMB	TCP, UDP	Microsoft Directory Services: TCP for Active Directory, Windows shares; UDP for Server Message Block (SMB) file-sharing
464	Kerberos	TCP, UDP	For password settings on Kerberos

547	DHCPv6	TCP, UDP	DHCPv6 Servers and DHCPv6 Relay Agents listen for DHCPv6 messages on UDP port 547.
596	SMSD	TCP, UDP	SysMan Station daemon
636	LDAP over TLS/SSL	TCP, UDP	Lightweight Directory Access Protocol over TLS/SSL
1720	H.323	TCP	H.323 Call Control Signaling, a VoIP call control protocol
3389	RDP	TCP	Windows Remote Desktop Protocol (Microsoft Terminal Server)
5060	SIP	TCP, UDP	Session Initiation Protocol
5061	SIP-TLS	TCP	Session Initiation Protocol over TLS

www.ingramcontent.com/pod-product-compliance
Lightning Source LLC
LaVergne TN
LVHW041214050326
832903LV00021B/614